ADVA

"'My Song, Unleashed' is a delightful memoir about love, loss, compassion and finding one's own path in life. Born into a large, well-known Minneapolis family, Marnie's place in the world seemed almost preordained. Yet, it's only when Marnie's journeys take her away from her family and out in the world that she begins to find her voice and learn to trust her innate wisdom. Reading 'My Song, Unleashed' is like chatting with a close friend. Not only will you be rooting for Marnie through the pages of this memoir, her wisdom will help you lean into your own. A lovely read!"

—Kate Hopper, author of "Ready for Air" and "Use Your Words"

"In her strong, gracious memoir, 'My Song, Unleashed,' Marnie Marmet deftly explores the enormous challenges she faced on her lifelong journey to wellness in mind, body and spirit. Every page is moving, poignant, and at times humorous and uplifting, too. Wise and motivating, 'My Song, Unleashed' is a memoir about the journey toward wholeness."

—Joelle Fraser, author of "The Territory of Men" and "The Forest House"

"Candid and compelling, Marnie's quest to discover her purpose is relatable to anyone on a journey. It's a great reminder that everyone has a story, and if you take the time to explore openly and honestly, you'll unlock deeper meaning and find your true voice."

—**Allison Kaplan, editor-in-chief**, **Twin Cities Business Magazine**

"Not only is this a compelling memoir, Marnie really opened up a vein and truly shared her story. Her 'song' is a lesson in vulnerability, and a master class in owning your truth."

—**Jordana Green, radio host, WCCO AM**

"What a pleasure to read 'My Song, Unleashed.' Marnie shares the highs and lows of her journey, examining how she has stumbled, coped and triumphed through formative moments of her life, with such warmth and raw honesty. You'll find yourself laughing and crying and cheering her on the whole way through."

—**Beth Lipton, author of "Carnivore-ish"**

My Song, Unleashed

a memoir

Marnie Dachis Marmet

PUBLISH **HER**™

Thank you so much for all of your support! Happy Reading!

MY SONG, UNLEASHED

© Copyright 2023 Marnie Dachis Marmet

All rights reserved. No portion of this book may be reproduced, stored in a retrieval system, or transmitted in any form or by any means—electronic, mechanical, photocopy, recording, scanning, or other—except for brief quotations in critical reviews or articles, without the prior written permission of the publisher.

This book is memoir. It reflects the author's present recollections of experiences over time. Some names and characteristics may have been changed, some events may have been compressed, and some dialogue may have been recreated.

Company and/or product names referenced in this book may be logos, trade names, trademarks, and/or registered trademarks, and are the property of their respective owners.

ISBN: 979-8-9865220-8-1 (Softcover)
Printed in the United States of America
First Printing: 2023

Published by Publish Her, LLC
2909 South Wayzata Boulevard
Minneapolis, MN 55405
www.publishherpress.com

Author photo by Belén Fleming

PUBLISH HER™

To Zach, Sage and Gabi:
This story is for you.

I want to sing like the birds sing, not worrying about who hears or what they think.

—RUMI

**What will you do with your one
wild and precious life?
—MARY OLIVER**

When I was in the sixth grade, I tried out for a special choir at my school called The Choristers. I loved to sing at home, and all my friends and the cute boys at school were going to be in it. I did not make the cut, and was instead placed in general music—a class for kids with no musical talent, no piano training, no instruments, nothing. It was humiliating. But that wasn't the end of it. The choir teacher took it a step further and called my mom out of concern; she recommended having a doctor check my vocal chords.

My mom didn't seem at all worried about my voice but she took me to see a specialist who looked in my throat and examined me.

"There is nothing wrong with her," he said with a laugh, addressing my mom as if I were invisible. "That's just her voice—scratchy sounding. That's how she talks and sings."

Thoughts of my dad referring to me as "The Rasp" echoed in my head.

"She won't be a professional singer," the doctor added, as if it wasn't already obvious.

Now two adults had declared that my singing voice was terrible. I wanted to get out of there as fast as possible.

I don't remember my mom contradicting the doctor or telling me I sounded OK. Instead, it became a joke in our family. She didn't have the best voice herself and it was something that bonded us.

My raspiness subsided in my teens, but the idea of a "terrible voice" stayed with me through adulthood. How do you find your voice when you have been silenced for so long? How do you learn that what you have to say is important, that your stories matter?

**Once we accept our limits,
we go beyond them.
—ALBERT EINSTEIN**

One of the first times I trusted and publicly used my voice was during my senior year of high school. A capstone graduation requirement was to write and give a senior speech in front of the entire school on any topic of the student's choosing. Some kids spoke about politics or traveling. Some spoke about a personal passion like ballet. Some gave a persuasive speech about subject matter like abortion. I decided to write about a personal experience: my dad going through drug and alcohol treatment three years earlier.

Only one of my closest friends knew that my dad had been in treatment. I worried about sharing the big secret publicly. What would people think of me, of my family? But I wanted to finally explain to my classmates why I never drank or used drugs at parties, and why I chose to be the designated driver. I wanted my classmates to know I had a reason for my choices. I was gripped by fear that I would become an alcoholic or drug addict if I tried anything and end up like my dad. Or worse, like Robert Downey, Jr. in the movie "Less Than Zero." I wanted to own my truth. No more lying to myself, or others. My inner voice was ready to burst out.

Growing up, I was part of a large, fun and loving extended family. I was a Dachis, and that meant something in my tightly knit Jewish community in Minneapolis, Minnesota. My dad was the oldest of seven kids who spanned 22 years. His youngest brother, Jeff, was only six years older than me, and was more like a brother than an uncle. The original "Dachis Seven," as they called themselves, were a rowdy bunch with six boys and one girl. Most of my uncles and my aunt went on to have one or two kids of their own, which meant I had many first cousins. Everywhere I went in the city, my last name was recognized. I loved the feeling and walked around with pride. Our name held so much meaning for me and represented my view of a perfect family. I'd heard someone say, "All you really have is your name, so honor it well and keep it honest," and I agreed wholeheartedly.

My brother and I were the oldest grandchildren, so we had weekly sleepovers with my grandparents, who everyone called Baubie and Zadie, the Yiddish names for grandma and grandpa. We often traveled with them, and they attended many of our school events. I loved going to their white colonial house with black trim on West 28th Street in St. Louis Park, a suburb of Minneapolis, for our large Friday night dinners. They had a huge backyard that sloped downward and was dotted with apple trees at the bottom of the hill. Baubie always made Kraft macaroni and cheese just the way I liked it—noodles and butter only, no cheese. I loved that Baubie paid special attention to how I liked my noodles.

I also had two loving parents, a nice two-story house in the suburbs, food on the table, fashionable clothes, regular family vacations, and a wonderful education at a private high school. My parents worked hard to get to where they were.

From a young age, I was incredibly attached to my cool, yellow Corvette-driving mom. My dad often joked about how I hung limply onto her leg as she dragged me around with her. I felt safe with her and wanted to be exactly like her. Others were envious of me and my mom—so close, like two sisters. She was one of the strongest women I knew, the rock of our family, the fun of our family.

My mom had had a rough childhood. Her dad

died unexpectedly of a heart attack when she was 14. Her older brothers and sister were grown and already out of the house, leaving my mom alone with her mother, who struggled with depression. She grew up in a rough neighborhood in Minneapolis, and money was always a struggle. She wanted to give my older brother, Louie, and me the best. When Guess jeans were popular, she bought me a pair in every color, even yellow, but the light pink ones were my favorite. I felt so lucky. I collected Mrs. Grossman's stickers, which were extremely popular in the '80s. Each week I'd go with my mom to our local grocery store, Byerly's, and we would stop at the boutique next store, Chrissy's Closet. That's where I would get new stickers for my collection, often the scratch and sniff type, and sometimes even some new, hip clothes.

My dad, while not super involved in my daily life, was my greatest champion at home. He always believed in me, even when I did not believe in myself, saying things like, "Marnie, we don't try, we do," or "You can do or become whatever you want."

In eighth grade, the crystalline image of my perfect family began to show cracks. I would hear my parents screaming at each other behind their closed bedroom door. When they finished, I would always ask, "Are you guys going to get a divorce?" After a while, this annoyed them both so much that they would often shout "NO!" in unison. I knew something was amiss, I just didn't know what it was.

My dad worked late many nights and didn't have a lot of time for me. My brother spent most of his time in his bedroom with different girls inside and the door locked. My mom would pound on his door, which had a fake plastic dirty diaper hanging on it, and other creepy stickers and things.

"Louie, let me in!" she would scream at the top of her lungs.

Inside his room he had a used condom tower. Punk rock posters and disturbing drawings he'd created covered every square inch of his walls. He also had a python named Spike. Once, Spike got out of the cage in Louie's room and ended up in my bed. I was traumatized for months.

My bedroom was next to Louie's, and walking from his room to mine was like walking from darkness into light. My mom let me pick out everything myself, and I loved the process of decorating my room. I had lavender carpet and paint-splattered wallpaper in aqua, hot pink and purple—my three favorite colors at the time (it was the '80s, after all). I had a queen brass bed and shelves that showcased all my Madame Alexander collector dolls, Santa Bears and other stuffed animals and trophies. My window overlooked the backyard and our hot tub. One of my favorite activities was spying on Louie when he brought a girl into the hot tub for a make-out session. I had the perfect angle through my thin, bendy metal window blinds, and could peer down at them without anyone knowing. Sometimes I would even crack my window and listen to their conversations.

Still, there was an undercurrent of stress in our daily lives. I felt it the moment I walked in the door from school. By ninth grade it had escalated. My brother was a senior in high school, and he drove me to school daily. He rarely spoke to me as we raced down the freeway in his hipster Jeep Wrangler with the Beastie Boys blasting "Brass Monkey."

Walking past me in the halls, Louie never even glanced my way, let alone said hello. As a freshman, I felt crushed by this, and longed for a sister or a sibling with whom I could have conversation or commiserate over our homework.

One afternoon in early May, a few days after my 15th birthday, my mom said she had to speak to me about something serious. My heart dropped. I was sure my parents were getting a divorce. It all made sense—the screaming, my dad's late nights at the office, the tension that had infused our once light-hearted home.

We stood in the kitchen, the afternoon sunlight pouring through the windows.

"Marnie, your dad has a drug and alcohol problem," my mom said gently. Her brown eyes looked so sad.

"What?" I asked in disbelief. "How can that be possible?"

I had seen my dad drink his martini straight up with green olives every evening at dinner, but I never remembered seeing him drunk. And a drug problem? My mom was nuts! And I was naive. Aside from drinking a few wine coolers in my friend's basement, I had little experience with alcohol at that point. I thought it was fun to pretend to be drunk after sipping the fruity wine coolers, but that was it. Some of my other friends had experimented with more, but I wasn't interested.

I had always been uncomfortable and embarrassed when my dad joked around with my friends about boys we liked or made flirtatious and bordering-on-inappropriate comments to waitresses when we had dinner at TGI Fridays, our family favorite. But wasn't every teen embarrassed by their dad?

My shock had not even slightly worn off before my mom said, "We're going to have an intervention."

"A what?" I asked, my mouth parched as I stared at our family photos across the room.

"An intervention," she said, as if repeating it made it clearer. "All your uncles are coming over. We're going to pretend we're having a celebration for your birthday. He'll come home in time for family dinner. He won't think twice about all the cars in the driveway."

I pictured the driveway and road dotted with familiar cars, my dad expecting a celebration and stepping into something else. I started to cry, tears streaming down my face, snot running everywhere.

"I don't want to be a part of it," I cried. "What if he blames me for tricking him into believing he was coming home for my birthday?"

I began to choke, feeling the weight of the world on my slender ninth grade shoulders. Why me? Why my family? How could this be happening to me? What would my friends think? What would people say? My birthday was going to be ruined forever. My mom didn't know what she was talking about.

"How do you know he has a problem?" I demanded, narrowing my green eyes at her.

"Buzzy suspected it for a while. He ran into your

dad a few days ago at the gas station downtown, and there was some strange behavior. And there are other things that I don't want to get into right now. But Marnie—" She paused. "I found cocaine in the bedroom cabinet. This is very real," she said, softer now, finally looking past her own pain to notice mine.

"COCAINE?!" I shouted. How could that be? My dad was not a druggie. There was no possible way.

Then I thought of all the hours he spent in our basement staring at the huge fish tank and telling us he was "spending time" with the fish. That was odd behavior. For the most part, though, what I noticed was his absence. He didn't attend my gymnastics meets or other activities, but my mom didn't go, either. My parents liked to do their own thing. They didn't engage much with my friends' parents or the PTA. Although this often left me feeling like I didn't matter, it was how it had always been.

I went through the following day in a fog. That night, as my uncles gathered at our home and came up with a plan, I stood in the corner of the dining room, my arms pulled tightly into my body as I memorized the parquet pattern on our wood flooring. I felt like I was going to vomit. I was practically choking on my breath.

I heard the garage door slowly open and my dad's convertible drive in. He sailed into the house, loud and chipper, "I'm home!" I stayed hidden in the dining room—I did not want to witness his realization that there was no birthday dinner for me.

I peeked around the corner, still out of sight, my stomach gripped by anxiety.

"What is going on here?" my dad demanded, his cheerful mood changing like an unexpected thunderstorm. Most of the family was piled together on the sectional in the family room—uncles, my grandmother, my mom and brother—arms crossed, primed for the intervention.

"Gary, you need help," Mom said firmly. "I know what is going on, that you're using alcohol and cocaine. It has become a major problem in our lives and our marriage. You have to go to treatment."

"You don't know what you're talking about," my dad thundered. "I don't have a problem and I don't use cocaine." His face was red. I tiptoed over and watched everything unfold.

My mom whipped out the bag of cocaine and hurled it at him. "Then what is this?" she screamed. "I found it in your dresser this morning, and I am going to flush it straight down the toilet right now!"

"Don't do that!" my dad yelled, furious. "Do you know how much money that's worth?"

I had heard them fighting through their bedroom door, but this—seeing them scream at each other—was different. I thought I might throw up.

"I don't care!" she yelled and ran into the bathroom.

Then we heard the flush of the toilet. I was sobbing, but no one noticed me. All eyes were on my dad, who stood with his fists clenched.

My uncle Buzzy piped up and explained that they had enrolled my dad in a 30-day inpatient program in downtown Minneapolis.

"There is no way I am going to an inpatient treatment program," my dad exclaimed, "I don't have a problem."

He started to negotiate with the family. "Maybe I will pop in for some meetings, but I need to come home to sleep at night and have my own space."

"You either do the inpatient program," my mom said, "or you leave us. Those are your options."

My brother, Louie, stood up, arms crossed in front of his chest, thick black eyeliner encircling his eyes, chains hanging from his pants. "I want my dad back."

Fear gripped my entire body. What if he left us? What if he chose drugs over his family?

"I need to think," Dad huffed. "I'm going to take a walk."

Before anyone could object, he took off, slamming the door behind him. It was a beautiful spring day, and it was finally staying light later into the evening. Everyone was shouting, making plans, gesturing, interrupting, but I was tuning them out. How had my life become so complicated? I just wanted my dad to come back.

Finally, after a walk and some thinking, my dad returned. "I'll go," he said, matter-of-factly. "But I'm coming home on the weekend and I'm doing this on my own terms."

My mom, uncles and grandparents exchanged knowing glances. There would be no coming home on the weekends with an inpatient program. Relief swept through my body. My dad was not going to leave us. But then, just as swiftly, reality set in. What would I tell my friends? What would people think? How could this be happening to my perfect family?

My dad started inpatient treatment at St. Mary's Hospital in Minneapolis the next day. It was not a plush facility like the Hazelden Betty Ford Drug Treatment Center, which was known for taking care of the wealthy. St. Mary's had patients from all walks of life, including homeless people.

I went back to school as a normal ninth grader the next day, but I was a total train wreck. I was exhausted, with dark circles under my eyes. It felt like everyone was staring at me, whispering and talking behind my back. "She's the girl whose dad is a druggie," I imagined. "My parents won't let me hang out around Marnie, because her dad is a lowlife who uses drugs."

I was ashamed of my family for the first time in my life, and I was behaving like I was a criminal or guilty of some terrible act. By the end of what had been a grueling day, one of my close friends noticed my extreme quietness, a departure from my usual bubbliness.

"What is going on with you today?" she asked, her large brown eyes concerned.

In that moment, I was thankful to have a friend, and I let down my guard. Everything poured out of me like a river.

"Promise me you will not tell your parents," I begged. "I don't want them to think badly of my dad. And promise me you won't tell anyone else. I am trusting you."

"I won't," she promised. And she didn't.

I wanted to see my dad while he was in treatment, but I hated making the 25-minute drive to a part of the city where I didn't feel safe. The car ride with Louie and my mom was uncomfortably silent, everyone lost in their own thoughts and pain. We would park and stand awkwardly outside on the sidewalk for a quick visit with my dad. All the patients stood there, near the parking ramp, meeting with their families and smoking. I hated cigarette smoke. When I was much younger, I would hold my nose and dramatically walk by smokers, giving them the stink eye. Now, my own dad had taken up smoking because it was helping him detox from the other chemicals he was addicted to. Another thing for me to be embarrassed about. Nobody else's parents smoked. Dad told us how he traded a pack of his cigarettes with another patient, and she would make his bed each day. I guess he had enough on his plate just trying to get clean.

The next time we came for a visit, my dad proudly zoomed a new remote-controlled toy car all over the sidewalk. He had earned a few hours of free time, and my mom told him he couldn't come home. So instead, he went to Target and bought himself the toy car.

My dad was assigned a sponsor and put into group therapy with many types of people. One quality I always admired in my dad was his ability to make friends with anyone. This helped him in treatment. He befriended a number of people he was getting to know in therapy. He was comfortably middle class, a hard-working, completely self-made man. But he always fit right in and related to people from all walks of life.

The third week of treatment was family week. This meant my mom, my brother and I were expected to attend sessions at the treatment center all week. I hated missing school, and that week happened to be finals week. I was devastated. How could I miss finals? My mom didn't seem to understand or care about the importance of my finals. She was more focused on my dad's recovery and the fact that we all needed to attend. She said she'd contact the school to let them know what was happening.

"No way!" I screamed. "You're not going to ruin my life at school. I do not want them to know. It is nobody's business!" I stared at her through teary eyes, hoping she would see how much this meant to me. "Please don't do this to me. Just tell them we have a private family situation that you cannot talk about."

That's what she did. My mom kept the secret. She understood my pain; she felt the same. The friend I'd told about my dad's addiction also kept my secret, even lying on my behalf when other friends asked why I wasn't in school.

I was terrified to go to family week. I had no idea what to expect, other than what my mom told me—I would have an opportunity to share whatever feelings I wanted with my dad, and I would be supported when I told him how I felt. That sounded really scary.

I thought back to the Saturdays when I was in elementary school and junior high when my dad and I would go running together through the trails in our neighborhood. He coined one of the steep hills "Heartbreak Hill," and we took pride in running straight to the top, arms pumping. During our runs, Dad would give me pep talks about whatever was on my mind. Whether it was advice on schoolwork, problems with friends, or work ethics, he peppered me with wisdom and encouraged me to go after what I wanted. He believed I could do anything. Now it was my turn. Dad clearly needed my support. I would encourage him to clean up his life and come home to us.

On that first day, I walked into the cold room and saw people sitting on metal folding chairs in a circle. Weariness hung in the air. It was a group therapy session with the families of other patients. I wanted to slink under my chair and wished I was invisible. I couldn't believe this was my life.

As the week progressed, each of us received individual counseling on mental health issues, trauma, grief, overcoming communication barriers, improving family dynamics, and effective coping strategies. I realized that the other families were in the exact same boat as ours. We were not alone. I didn't say much in the group sessions, but I heard everything—I soaked it all in and took it to heart.

I learned an entirely new vocabulary. Words like "junkie," "chemical dependency," "codependency" and "AA." The counselors taught us facts about drugs and alcohol, how addiction is a disease, and how it can be treated and managed, but not cured. There were many different meetings. Always with cold, hard chairs arranged in a circle, and always the smell of cigarette smoke clinging to the residents' clothing.

I was the youngest person in the room—other families didn't bring their kids to family week. But my family was close-knit, and my mom would never have thought to exclude me, Louie, my uncles or my grandparents.

I learned my mom was codependent as our counselor explained what codependency and enabling looked like. I realized when we were sheltering or protecting my dad, we were also protecting our own feelings. My mom was emotionally connected to the ups and downs of my dad, and that took away her identity, integrity and happiness.

Things started to make sense to me. Even though I was angry with my dad, I also wanted to protect him. I wanted to come up with excuses for why he got himself into this situation. Perhaps his work was too stressful. Maybe he worried too much about money. But what I really learned over the next few days, directly from my dad, was that from a young age, he did not feel good inside. He felt pressure to be perfect. Him too?

He started to experiment with various highs at age 15 and got used to and comfortable with himself under the influence. It was easier to be what he thought was himself when he was high. I felt so sad as he choked up. It was the moment I promised myself I would not let it happen to me. I would not go down the same road. I understood that I might have an addictive personality and it was not worth the risk. I vowed to never use drugs and not to drink until I was of legal age.

The counselor who worked with me one on one

was empathetic and gentle, like a big-bearded teddy bear. We sat on folding chairs facing one another, and he asked how I felt about my dad and everything that had happened. I did not know any of the signs of addiction and had been clueless until my mom sprang the news on me. When I was younger, Dad would come into my room nightly and talk to me through my stuffed animals. He would take Scarlet O'Beara and Humphrey Beargart off a shelf and say, "How was your day, Marnie? Anything to share? Goodnight and sweet dreams." Sometimes he would ramble on and on and what he said made no sense. I found it comforting and funny at the same time. Looking back on those memories, I hoped my dad was sober, but I wasn't sure.

I told the counselor I felt ashamed and disappointed in my dad. It was my dad who had told me not to try or use drugs and alcohol. I listened to him. I adored him and wanted to make him proud.

On the last day of family week, it was time to tell Dad how we felt. It was just our family in the room, and as had been the custom all week, we started the meeting with the serenity prayer: "God grant me the serenity to accept the things I cannot change, the courage to change the things I can and the wisdom to know the difference."

I found the prayer comforting, and I contemplated its meaning.

Next, we went around the room and Baubie spoke first about her feelings and her disappointment in my dad. Everyone was sobbing by the end of her revelations, including my dad. He was ashamed of his behavior in front of his parents. He was their first-born son and took his role seriously. He hated that he had let them and his siblings down.

When it was my turn, I shared my truth.

"I am so disappointed in you, Dad. I trusted and I believed in you. You were one of my greatest role models, and my faith in you is gone."

I cried like a baby, releasing everything from my tight body, and he cried along with me. I felt knotted up seeing how awful it made my dad feel. But I also felt a sense of relief. There was some extra space in my chest—a place where I tend to hold emotion—for me to breathe again. Later I would realize the power in speaking one's truth, not just in moments of crisis, but in everyday life.

My mom took her turn and so did my brother. Louie was especially harsh. Because he was older, he had experienced more disappointment and, in some ways, had taken it even harder than I had. They had a rockier relationship, but I knew Dad loved us both fiercely.

By the end of the week, life was lighter. I couldn't believe how well communication worked. I had always thought we were a communicative bunch, but what we had just experienced was an entirely new level. Everything was on the table. My dad was doing really well, and he was about ready to come home. This meant my parents would have to change their entire life—make new friends, drop their partying friends, spend four or five nights a week attending AA meetings together and separately.

I started going to meetings with my mom and dad once a week on Thursday nights. I loved this tradition. I would go to Al-Anon with my mom and my dad would go to his own meeting. I felt safe in these meetings as I listened to others share their stories. We would go out to dinner at TGI Fridays afterward. I would order nachos with the cheddar cheese melted in a perfect triangle and topped off with a green jalapeno on each flat chip.

I took my final exams by myself, one week into summer break. Nobody questioned it; my friends were off running around in the sunshine having fun. I hadn't shared the details of my dad's addiction with more of my friends. Word had gotten out in the Jewish community, though no one said anything directly to me about it. My once very social parents were home every night. We read books and played intense Scrabble games on the screen porch when the humidity of summertime was thick. We drove around Lake Harriet in my dad's convertible, stopping for buttery popcorn at the bandstand. We spent a lot of wonderful family time together. Mom stopped drinking entirely to support Dad and to keep our house dry. My relationship with Louie started to change for the better. Our experience had brought us closer, and he seemed to sense I needed a brother. He started taking more of an interest in me, and we talked more.

Thinking back to this time, I realize how much I learned about myself, my family dynamics and relationships. Family week was intensive therapy, and it truly taught me how to communicate my feelings clearly and publicly. Many people joke about Minnesotans being passive-aggressive and keeping our feelings bottled up with niceties. But I learned at a young age how to throw it all out on the table and not keep anything inside. If we had something to say, we said it. There were no more secrets. I began confiding in friends and sharing what was going on in my life. These skills would carry forward into my adult life and impact how I raised my own children.

It was what I learned during family week that helped prepare me for my senior capstone speech. As I stepped onto the stage, I gripped my note cards. I had rehearsed the speech so many times in front of the dining room mirror at home that I had it memorized. I had practiced my posture, how to look directly into the eyes of an audience member, and how to clearly emphasize certain words. I spotted my parents in the back row and locked eyes with my dad—I knew I could do it.

My voice shook in the beginning and grew stronger. The audience was so quiet you could hear a pin drop. Students leaned forward, genuinely engaged in my story, and I felt empowered. By the time I finished, the entire room was standing and applauding loudly. I felt euphoric; my secret was out, off my chest and into the world. I had nothing left to hide.

My dad shared years later how hard it was for him to be in the audience listening to my speech. Not only did it bring back so many painful memories, but he was also embarrassed; it had been something like a public humiliation. He felt it had been his penance to be there and sit tall, despite wanting to crawl under his chair and hide. He was also very proud of me.

The rest of that day at school I received many congratulations from students and teachers. A few students approached me and shared that they had a parent recovering from an addiction as well. It felt so good to share my story, to connect with other kids who could relate, and to feel less alone through my words.

The biggest compliment I received was the principal letting me know they recorded my speech and asking if they could share it with future students each year in health class. Of course, I said yes. And my dad has remained sober for more than 30 years, never once having a relapse.

It takes courage to grow up and become who you really are.
—E.E. CUMMINGS

As a teenager, I never liked to sleep away from home except when I was at Herzl Camp, my favorite summer camp in Wisconsin. When I hung out with my friends on the weekends, they would either sleep at my house, or once I had my license, I would drive home by my self-imposed midnight curfew. I was a homebody, and though I loved to be social, I was also quite content hanging out with my parents. They were home a lot after my dad got sober. I enjoyed relaxing on our wooden screened porch, each of us immersed in our own books or listening to and watching summertime thunderstorms. I loved the smell of the hot, humid nights mixed with the rain.

When it was time to think about college, I decided with the help of my college counselor that I wanted to visit the University of Vermont and Boston University—two completely different schools I had chosen while paging through catalogs I received in the mail.

Mom and I flew out to Boston the spring of my junior year, and after a quick tour, I was certain Boston University was not the school for me. It was way too "city" for me and there was not a separated campus, but rather a few blocks of buildings in the heart of Boston. I loved how the Charles River ran through Boston and the vibrant city life, but I could not see myself spending four years there.

The next day, Mom and I packed up and drove three and a half hours to Burlington, Vermont. As I looked out the window at all the farmlands passing by, I started to have doubts about the University of Vermont as well. I would have to fly to Boston and drive three hours every time I needed to get to school or to return home from school. This was sounding less and less appealing. When we checked into a cheap hotel in Vermont and I turned on the TV, all of the stations were in French. French! How far away from home was I? I hadn't realized how close we were to the Canadian border.

"Mom, I don't think I want to visit the university tomorrow anymore," I explained, feeling on edge and nervous. "I'd like to go back to Boston tomorrow instead.

"What?" my mom asked with wide eyes. "We just drove over three hours to get here."

"I know," I said, truly sorry, "But I'm sure I don't want to go to school here. It's way too far from home and they speak French on all the local TV stations."

It took me visiting Boston and driving to Vermont to realize that these schools were too far from home for my comfort, and I was not ready to leave my nest. Mom didn't question me or even insist we go on the tour. Perhaps she didn't want me to be that far away either.

The next morning, we drove past the campus and skipped the tour, not even getting out of our rental car. Instead, we stopped at the original Ben & Jerry's store and got ice cream, and then headed back to Boston to explore and shop.

Later that summer, I decided to apply to the University of Wisconsin-Madison. It was a four hour drive from our house to the university campus. Close enough that I could come home for a weekend, yet far enough away that I could have my own college experience. This felt better to me.

When I went to college that fall, after two days of unpacking and getting settled, my parents left me in my freshman year dorm room at The Towers. My single room was decorated with a pastel comforter, and photos of my friends and family dotted my walls. I didn't have a roommate—I had a suite mate, a girl from Long Island, New York. We shared a sparse bathroom and a mini kitchen, but each had our own private rooms. In retrospect, I think I would have preferred a roommate.

As I sat alone in my room, I began to feel sick to my stomach. I was in total shock that this was my new room, my new life. I felt like I was on a spinning ride that would not stop. I ran to the bathroom and threw up, something I hadn't done since I had the stomach flu as a young kid. Then I picked up the receiver on my pink wall phone and dialed my dad's car phone—it was one of those bulky ones that sat in the middle console.

"I just threw up," I cried into the phone. "What if I'm sick on my first day of college?" How will I meet anyone?" Tears streamed down my face.

"You won't believe this. We had to pull over because your mom just threw up," dad said. "You are both incredibly sad and anxious about leaving each other. You are two peas in a pod."

At that, I realized just how connected we were. Dad had always called us "the mother-daughter combo." Listening to him calmed me.

"Why don't you go find a friend from home like Amy or Ellie and do something to take your mind off leaving home?" my parents suggested.

My mom and I both laughed through our tears and said our I love yous and goodbyes. I would do my best to cut the cord a little at a time.

I called Ellie and asked if she'd like to knock on doors and meet some of the other kids on each of the floors in the dorm. She was in my room within minutes, her bouncy blond hair, high-pitched laugh and warm smile bringing me right into the moment.

All my fears were forgotten as we stepped into the hallway and knocked on our first door. It swung open and there stood a handsome guy who looked younger than college-aged. He was wearing a black surfing T-shirt and had olive skin and warm brown eyes that crinkled in the corners when he smiled.

"Hi, I'm Jordan," he said. "I'm from California."

"Hi!" Ellie and I said at the same time.

This should be interesting, I thought. "Cute boy next door" alert bells sounded in my head.

A month into school, Jordan and I had our first hook-up, and we eventually started dating officially. We broke up many times. Our relationship was immature. Even as we became more serious about each other over time, we behaved like 18- and

19-year-olds. We didn't know how to address our conflicts and would break up whenever we were angry, only to get back together a few days later.

But Jordan also showed me how to fold laundry and cook. He taught me to balance a checkbook and understand credit and loans. He encouraged me to sign up for my first credit card to build credit in my name. He had grown up in a very different household and had learned many of these skills at a young age. He was making his own school lunches by the second grade, which shocked me. "My mom was still making my peanut butter and jelly sandwiches during my senior year, when I worked at a summer day camp," I told him sheepishly.

I continued to rely on my mom for emotional support and friendship all through college. She knew my deepest, darkest secrets and worries. And I worried about everything. Would I be successful enough? Would I get into a sorority? Would I meet friends? But by the time I graduated, Jordan and I were seriously dating, and we decided to move into an apartment together instead of me moving back to my parents' house.

I wasn't entirely sure how I really felt about this, but I went along with it since Jordan was moving to Minnesota for me. I liked how I felt when I was with him. We were total opposites in many ways. He was a calming presence in my life. Nothing rattled him; everything seemed to rattle me. He was also deeply smart and well read. I was attracted to this. We could engage in hours of deep conversation, and I always learned something from him. He was so different from my dad, my brother and the other men in my life, and I liked how he took care of me. He also understood that I was sensitive. In college, he made me mix tapes of music he loved from Def Leppard and Guns N' Roses and write me beautiful cards as we celebrated our monthly anniversaries.

We rented an apartment a mile from my parents' house, which made it easy to run home too often. I was actually living in an apartment with my boyfriend, making dinners, paying bills, arranging furniture, yet I still felt like a child inside. My life was not quite my own. My mom's opinion mattered too much, and I looked to her to validate what I wore, what I should cook for dinner and more. Though I had learned about codependency while my dad was in treatment, I didn't yet see the ways my relationship with my mother was still completely codependent. I continued to seek her approval. And each time she said, "You should put a little lipstick on to brighten up your face," or "I like your hair better blonder," I internalized it, which often left me feeling inadequate and unattractive.

Still, I was determined to make my way in the world. My first job after college was with the buying program at Dayton's corporate headquarters. Dayton's was an American department store chain founded in Minneapolis in 1902 by George Draper Dayton. When I was younger, going shopping downtown at Dayton's was a special experience anytime, but especially around the holidays. My mom, Baubie and I would park in the giant ramp. We would start with lunch in the restaurant on the top floor where they served melt-in-your-mouth popovers. I would always wear a special dress. Then we'd go to the eighth floor to see the animated Christmas show (even though we were Jewish). There was a different theme each year such as Cinderella, The Grinch, The Nutcracker, and even Harry Potter in later years. Dayton's turned itself into a magical place. It was a pillar of our community.

I graduated with a Bachelor of Arts in journalism with an emphasis in marketing and public relations, and a concentration in business. I had sent my resume to a number of potential employers, and Dayton's was one of the first to contact me. I was excited because it was a highly sought-after and competitive position.

After multiple interviews, I received a generous offer—more than I had imagined I would earn right out of college—and it came with amazing benefits, including a standing discount at all Target and Dayton's stores. This discount alone would be helpful, as Jordan and I needed to buy all the furnishings for our new and mostly empty apartment. And I was enamored with the idea of going downtown every day, buying cute new work outfits and a feminine Coach briefcase.

I took the job without a clear understanding of what I would be doing. But I would start in the training program, which would teach me whatever I needed to know. My first two weeks on the job were overwhelming but fun. I was with the trainees from around the U.S., most of whom had relocated to Minneapolis for the position. We were handed large binders with all our materials, and we went from class to class learning about the history of the company and how different departments worked together.

In our second week, we dove into the buying process and started to get a better picture of what the job truly entailed—a lot of number crunching. I had imagined glamorous buying trips to New York and Paris, long fancy lunches and being surrounded by trendsetters all day.

Clearly, I was off base.

I was assigned to work in the china department (plates and tableware). What? Seriously? I would work under a woman named Carrie who had short, dark hair cut into a style that communicated "I mean business." Her assistant in our pod, Alana, was a young blonde woman who was happy to work any number of hours and do exactly whatever Carrie barked at her, including fetching her coffee. I was not used to this dynamic, and I was disappointed to be placed in the china department. Most of my counterparts were working in ready-to-wear clothing. Their workspaces were on the opposite end of our floor in an area that housed row upon row of gray cubicles. You could get lost in there if you took a wrong turn. Alana advised me to always plan to arrive before Carrie in the morning, and stay in the evening until after Carrie left, no matter how late it was. It sounded horrible to me. I had envisioned driving home from my new hip job, meeting Jordan back at our cute apartment in the suburbs, hanging out and spending the evening experimenting with new recipes.

I wasn't interested in attending drawn-out,

drunken happy hours after the long workday. I had many friends in the area who were also coupled up—I had looked forward to double dating and checking out fun new restaurants.

By the end of my first week in the china department, I hated the job. Sitting in my drab cubicle with no windows anywhere nearby was sucking the life out of me. I sat idly at my desk, staring at my computer screen, interacting only with Alana when she had something to show or explain to me. Most of the job involved pouring over spreadsheets, which detailed long lists of purchase orders of all different patterns of china brands, like Damask, Noritake, Wedgwood, Lenox, Waterford and Mikasa.

I slogged through those gorgeous summer days, suffocating inside. My boss was flat-out mean. She would look down at me, glasses perched on her nose, and yell, "Marnie! Where are my numbers?" or "Have you called so-and-so vendor?" or "Go grab my lunch for me!"

Lunch was my favorite time of day. While Alana and Carrie remained chained to their desks, I explored the many skyways that connected the buildings in downtown Minneapolis. I walked past lunch spots, coffee shops, musicians and people rushing everywhere. It was as if the streets of New

York City were bottled up into the skyways. I loved the energy and the people-watching and would just walk and walk.

Sometimes I headed to the outdoor plaza of Nicollet Mall, where on Thursdays there was always a farmers market. On those days, I would roam around the fresh produce, inhaling the wonderful scents and purchasing fresh flowers for our apartment. This 30-minute break was my lifeline during those long days. I liked my coworkers from the training program, but now that everyone was assigned to different departments, and since I typically skipped most of the happy hours to race home and connect with Jordan, I rarely saw them.

My spirit felt crushed on a daily basis. I thought a lot about how my career wasn't going the way I had hoped. I didn't have a good sense of what I wanted to do, but I was beginning to understand what I did not want to do—work my ass off in a large company at a job I hated, slowly climbing the ranks, aspiring to get my boss's unhappy job one day.

One weekend, Jordan and I went to my parents' house for a Sunday night family dinner.

"Marnie, we need to talk," my dad said.

"What's up?" I asked, wondering what it could be about.

"I'm proud of you for going out and getting this job, but clearly you are miserable." His eyes were concerned. "You're at a time in your life when you have a blank slate in front of you. Maybe you should think about doing something else." He paused. "You know, I had a similar experience in my first job out of college. I worked for Cargill, and I barely lasted six months before going out on my own."

"But what would I do? I don't even know anymore," I said, my voice shrill. How would I tell Carrie that I was quitting? I was not a quitter.

"Perhaps you can work in the family business until you figure it out," my dad said, like it was the most natural thing in the world. He reminded me that my brother, my brother's wife at the time, and my mom were all working at Game Financial Corporation, a business my father had started that provided check cashing and credit card advances to casinos around the country. Business was booming, and the company was growing fast. He told me to think about it.

That night I kept turning the idea over in my mind. I wasn't too keen on going into the family business. I was proud that I had found my own job. And our family dinners were already full of Game Financial business, business, business. But they did all seem to be having a lot of fun doing their jobs. Plus my dad was giving me an opportunity that might be too good to pass up.

After multiple conversations with Jordan, I decided to quit my job at Dayton's at the end of the training program. I would learn everything I could and make the best of it, knowing it would soon come to an end. My slate would be clean again. Dayton's would be a blip on the radar—one I might not even add to my resume. Though I would miss the employee discount.

When I gave my notice, Carrie barely looked me in the eye. I secretly imagined she was jealous that I was getting out. I knew she had two small children at home. I wondered if she ever spent any time with them, and what her home life was like. She rarely smiled and seemed to relish her role applying negative pressure on people beneath her.

On my last day, I turned in my badge, walked out the door and never looked back. I embarked on my new career at Game Financial.

Game Financial had a payroll person but no formal human resources department, so Dad suggested I develop the department from the ground up. I agreed, though I was disappointed I wouldn't be working in marketing, which was Louie's domain. My brother had transformed himself from an artist working in set design into a promising businessman, thriving in his marketing role and assisting in the company's explosive growth. And so, HR it was for me.

I spent the year hiring, firing and onboarding employees both locally and around the country, where new employees were embedded in GameCash storefronts in casinos. I developed all the company policies, procedures, manuals and standard practices. I enrolled in business classes in the evening to learn everything I could about how small companies can run more effectively. I learned about benefits administration and employee satisfaction, and I led the executive team in developing the company's mission and values statements. I learned so much, and most of it was self-taught.

I was the youngest person on the executive team and was often treated poorly by the other executives. My dad told me I'd have to work twice as hard because of who I was, so I did. I fought against the sideways glances and comments about nepotism and worked my butt off. I loved the job and the ways it challenged me. I discovered what I really enjoyed was the process of building and developing something from scratch.

My work life was finally going really well, and

then everything changed in my personal life. Jordan announced he'd decided to go to medical school halfway around the world in Tel Aviv, Israel. After much discussion, we agreed he would go there alone for the first year and I would stay in Minneapolis, working and taking graduate-level business classes. I had just been accepted into two business master's degree programs—one in Minneapolis at the University of St. Thomas, and the other at Northwestern University in Chicago. Plus, Jordan would need to focus on attending classes and studying endlessly. Eventually, if we could keep our long-distance relationship together, we'd get engaged and I would move to Tel Aviv with him.

While this made the most sense if we were going to spend the rest of our lives together, neither of us had given much thought to what it would be like once I joined him there. After Jordan officially enrolled in medical school abroad, I was too afraid to continue pursuing my own passions. Despite our earlier conversations, I felt I had to make a choice—my education, or Jordan and me.

Our long-distance relationship worked, Jordan proposed marriage, and I chose him and the big move to Israel. I did what many young women in my community were conditioned to do. It was what was expected of me and frankly, what I expected of myself. I saw friends getting married and ready to have babies; my brother and his wife were starting a family. My mom and Baubie both married young and became young mothers. I didn't key into my own wants or desires at the time, which wasn't that different from my mom's story—she gave up a career she loved as an aerobics instructor to work with my dad. She even had her own cable television show, Firm Up With Elaine, and she gave it up for the family business. But she was also from a different generation.

For years I would wonder why Jordan and I didn't discuss this further. Why didn't I pursue my own master's degree? Was it because I knew I wanted to be a stay-at-home mom at some point? Did I think furthering my education was a luxury and would not contribute much to our life together?

I had spent time in Tel Aviv previously, studying abroad during the second semester of my junior year of college. I'd had an incredible experience there, socializing, partying and embarking on elaborate yet college-aged thrifty adventures around the region. We went hiking and rappelling all over the country on the weekends. I developed my love for the outdoors during that time. I never expected to go back so soon, let alone move there to be with my future husband.

Jordan and I would get married in Minneapolis during the summer between his second and third years of medical school. I was nervous about the move. At the last minute, after I asked incessantly, my parents acquiesced and allowed me to bring the family dog, Sonya, with me. She was a Siberian husky-shepherd mix, with slightly crossed piercing blue eyes. She had been my comfort, my companion, since our dog Maggie died during my freshman year of high school. My dad and I went to the Humane Society the day after Maggie's death to "just look" at the dogs available for adoption—at least that's what we told my mom. She had forbidden us from coming home with a new dog. But when I saw Sonya's big sapphire eyes staring at me, I knew she was a gentle old soul. It was kismet. We brought her home and she became my new wonder mutt. Now Sonya would be flying to Israel.

"What?!" friends would ask in disbelief. "You're taking a dog to Israel with you?"

"Yes, I am," I responded. It was the only decision I felt confident about at the time.

Life begins at the end of your comfort zone.
—NEALE DONALD WALSCH

After many emotional goodbyes and exorbitant amounts of paperwork, I was on my way to Israel with Jordan. We'd purchased a giant kennel for Sonya, and she would be mildly sedated for the flight. It made me sad, but I knew it was the only way to get her there. We would fly from Minneapolis to Toronto and then switch planes and fly directly to Tel Aviv. We would be able to see Sonya in Toronto and take her out of the kennel to go to the bathroom and eat.

At the Air Canada check-in counter in Minneapolis, we had a problem.

"Your kennel is too large," the man with a crisp uniform and French accent said to us with a frown.

"What?" I shrieked. "I read all of the requirements and we followed everything to a T."

"We had an unforeseen plane change earlier today," he explained. "The aircraft is much smaller and does not have space in the cargo hold."

My nerves exploded. I could not leave without Sonya. She was a piece of home that I had to have with me. I needed her like a baby needs its stuffed lovey. My mom and dad had joined us at the airport to say goodbye. As my dad noticed I was about to burst into tears, he stepped up to the counter to help me. He told the attendant that I was moving out of the country, that we had a long journey ahead of us, and that Sonya must accompany us and make this next flight. I could almost hear the minutes ticking away. We were going to miss our flight.

"Dad," I whispered through my tears.

"Sha, Marnie," he said. "Let me handle this." He switched into full charmer mode and proceeded to sweet-talk the man behind the counter.

After a short wait, the man informed us he received special permission from the pilot, who happened to be a dog lover, for us to board the plane with Sonya if we sat in the very back row and kept her at our feet. Sonya weighed around 60 pounds. Though she often dropped her head casually into any available lap, she was no lap dog. But I wasn't about to argue with the pilot's compromise. I jumped and laughed and cried at the same time. There was no time to focus on goodbyes as we raced with Sonya to board the plane.

Anxiety raced through my veins as I thought about the remainder of our travels. I do recall the pilot paying a visit to the back of the small plane to see Sonya and welcome us aboard. She was in her drugged and drowsy state, but I was certain she was more comfortable snuggling up against our legs on the long flight than in the cold underbelly of the plane.

The rest of our trip to Israel was uneventful, and we eventually made it to the apartment in Tel Aviv. Jordan had rented it during his first year of school and I hadn't seen it ahead of time, so I was going to have to trust his judgment. From the outside, the building looked ancient. Dirt was caked on the plastered walls, and there were no screens on the windows. I noticed all the cats hanging out in the alleys near the garbage dumpsters. But there were also palm trees and flowers everywhere and the air smelled like orange blossoms.

It was late August when we arrived, and it was blazing hot. Jordan was proud that he had found a third-floor apartment that had an AC unit in the main sitting room. At first glance, the tiny, furnished apartment seemed nice. The couple that had lived there were studying in the U.S. and were renting it out. It had a small sitting area with a moderately comfortable black futon, an older TV and a chair.

The kitchen was connected to the sitting area by a hallway with a curved ceiling. It had an old, yellowed 1960s-style fridge, a few dirty cabinets and a stove top. There were dishes, silverware, glasses—everything we would need to get by. As I surveyed the kitchen where I would eventually learn to cook, an angry woman in the apartment above our heads yelled "Leveee!" followed by a string of words in Hebrew, which I didn't understand. Even though I had learned how to read and write Hebrew as a child in preparation for my bat mitzvah, I had a limited vocabulary, no grammar knowledge, and difficulty speaking and understanding the spoken language.

Off the kitchen, there was a porch with an outdoor laundry area. The machines looked decades old and were so dirty that I wondered if my clothes would actually come out clean. Down a short hallway, was a small office and the bedroom. What was considered a queen-sized bed was really a small double, more like a twin and a half. A large white electric fan rotated hot air around the room. As I took it all in, I felt disappointed and dismayed. Was this really my new reality? I was afraid to see the bathroom.

As I stepped back into the hallway, I noticed a button on the wall.

"What's this?" I asked Jordan.

"It's the switch you hit to heat up the water for the shower. There's a small water tank on the roof that heats up when the switch is flipped."

"I need to press a button to heat the water before I take a shower? EVERY DAY?!"

I felt like I had been transported into someone else's life. I thought about my friends back home, deep into their careers, planning weddings, living in swanky city apartments or buying starter houses in the suburbs. Years later I would realize how spoiled I was, and how a different mindset could have changed my entire perspective on the experience on which I was embarking. But I was still a sheltered girl in many ways. Now, part of me wanted to throw a tantrum like a child. Bang my fists, kick my feet and scream, "I want to go home!" But we had no landline phone, and cell phones were rare and expensive.

Getting a landline set up through the Israeli phone company was a multi-day affair at best—it was not a service-based economy like the U.S. During these first few days and weeks, I tried to hold it together for Jordan's sake. Whenever I wanted to call home, I'd quietly make my way down the multiple flights of stairs and out the building and walk to a pay phone down the block.

"Mom!" I'd cry into the phone. "I can't do this! Our apartment is awful." I did not yet realize how overindulged I was. I didn't think about how I must have sounded, to my mother and to Jordan.

My mission became making our apartment as comfortable as I could. Jordan was in class all day, so I tried to keep myself busy. I felt like an outsider. And I began to recognize how different it was to actually live in Israel compared to my studying abroad there as a carefree college student.

I was determined to settle into our new home and get to know the neighborhood. I went to the grocery store for the first time on a Thursday afternoon. I later learned that was the day most Israelis liked to shop, before the country closes down for the Sabbath, known there as shabbat. I entered the Supersol grocery store a few blocks from our home and saw no carts. I attempted with my limited Hebrish (a combination of Hebrew and English) to ask where I could find one. The answer finally came as a grunt and some hand motions, which I understood to mean I would have to grab one as someone else checked out. Once inside with a cart, I realized shopping was a game of "check." Pushy babushkas—old Russian women wearing head scarves—rammed their carts straight into mine to get past me. They jutted their elbows out as they raced by and hurried through their shopping. As I walked home in tears, the heavy plastic grocery bags cutting off the circulation in my fingers, I felt completely drained. But I knew I needed to figure out how to make it work.

Days later, as I deep-cleaned the kitchen in attempt to make the place homier, large black bugs began scampering and flying around the room. I realized the apartment had cockroaches (or "jukies," as Israelis called them).

"This place is infested with cockroaches! I cannot live here!" I shouted at Jordan when he returned from class.

He argued that there weren't many and we would get them cleaned up. There was nothing we could do about them flying in from the windows since there were no screens. That night, I struggled to sleep and when I did, I dreamt of bugs crawling into my eyes and ears and nose. I would jolt awake, disoriented, and realize I was in Tel Aviv, in my new apartment with Jordan.

My parents suggested we hire someone to clean our apartment and spray for cockroaches. We didn't have a lot of extra money to spare, but I thought it was a magnificent idea. Jordan did not. He was in denial there was a problem.

"I don't care what it costs," I announced a couple of days later. "It is essential for my sanity and happiness to live somewhere I feel comfortable."

I had Israeli cousins who helped me find an exterminator. When he came to spray the apartment, Sonya and I left for a walk for several hours. When we met Jordan back at the apartment later, I was afraid to enter. He walked in first and I tiptoed behind him. The first thing I noticed were all the open cabinet doors. And then hundreds upon hundreds of dead cockroaches. Everywhere.

"Now do you believe me?" I asked.

"You're right," Jordan nodded. "We clearly had a bug problem."

The exterminator told us he'd need to come back and spray one more time for it to fully work. He said often the jukies skitter over to the next apartment (at least the ones that were not poisoned to death). I shuddered at the thought of it.

Later that week, I met a few of Jordan's American and Canadian classmates and inquired about cleaning help. One of them gave me the name of a South American man named Manni who had cleaned for her at a reasonable rate. I called him. His native language was Spanish, and he spoke a little English and a little Hebrew. Jordan was fluent in Spanish, having studied it through high school and college. We hired Manni on the spot. He would come the next day, and then once every other week.

I started to settle into a routine. Jordan was in school five days a week, now in his second year of medical school, and had hours of studying to do when he came home. I had an abundance of free time on my hands and not much to do. I didn't like being alone with my thoughts and often felt tearful and sad. It was a lonely time. I was used to being busy and productive, working and being surrounded by family and friends. I felt like I was starting from scratch. I wondered what was going on with everyone back home. Had they forgotten about me halfway around the world?

I spent hours each day meandering the beautiful palm tree-lined streets with Sonya. I'd pet her and talk to her like she was my best friend. I was comforted by her presence. People regularly inquired what kind of breed she was. Most Israelis had little, yippy dogs that pooped on the sidewalks, so our big, gorgeous husky with blue eyes was an unusual sight. We explored and found many cute cafes to come back to another time for dinner. Marilyn

Monroe's, a cafe about a mile or two from home, became a favorite. The fresh pastas and fresh salads were mouth-wateringly delicious, and we loved the outdoor seating on the pretty sidewalk.

We didn't eat all of our meals out. I attempted to make matzo ball soup from scratch for the first time at our apartment—not an easy feat in an old-fashioned kitchen. I called my mom for our family recipe. I toiled over the stove using real chicken and skimming off the fat—schmaltz in Yiddish, which was what my grandparents called it. I dripped with perspiration as I focused on making the matzo balls perfectly firm, but not too firm, as my family liked them. The delicious smell of soup and the memory of the Jewish High Holidays at home wafted throughout our tiny apartment. My mouth watered as I stirred.

What I didn't account for was my mom's recipe being enough to serve 10 to 15 people. There were just the two of us in Israel, and we only had a small fridge with a tiny frosted-over freezer. What would we do with all the leftover soup? Jordan suggested we invite over some of his med school classmates to share it. I thought this was a great idea. We packed up the matzo ball soup I had labored over for hours and stuck the containers in the fridge. The next day, when I opened the refrigerator, it was barely running.

The food inside was spoiled. By midday the fridge had died completely.

Our landlords agreed to replace it, and I was so giddy with excitement I almost forgot the soup was ruined and we wouldn't have new friends over to eat it. When our "new" fridge arrived, it was puke green and a decade newer than the old one—still practically an antique. It was three-quarters the size of a standard American fridge. Not quite what I was hoping for, but better than nothing. I was starting to appreciate the little luxuries.

The suburb where we lived, Ramat Aviv, was near the university, and close to the dazzling blue Mediterranean Sea. I would often walk Sonya down to the Tel Baruch white sandy beach, a family beach by day, less family-friendly at nighttime. Sonya would tear around and nuzzle her snout deep in the sand and run into the waves. She was so joyful, racing all around. She had grown up around Minnesota lakes, and I imagined how she marveled at the majesty of the Mediterranean Sea.

Despite my efforts to get settled and stay busy, I was lonely and bored and hadn't figured things out for myself. I took out my frustrations on Jordan. I wanted more of his attention, which he couldn't give me with all of his classes and the amount of time he had to dedicate to studying. I had put all my eggs in his basket, which wasn't fair.

I decided to enroll in an "Ulpan," an immersive learning experience used in teaching Hebrew in Israel, typically for new immigrants and free for anyone interested in joining. It is based on three core principles: teach Hebrew in Hebrew, focus on practical skills, and introduce students to the culture. I found a class for immigrants who had recently made "Aliyah" to Israel (which literally means rising up but translates to moving to Israel). It was a five-minute walk from our apartment. The class met Sunday through Thursday from 9 a.m. to noon.

My first day, I was thrilled to understand everything that was spoken in the class. We sat in a semicircle in a hot classroom. There were about 15 students, mostly women ages 19 to 30, who came from all over the world—Germany, France, South America, Canada. I was the only person in the class from the U.S., and one of two who had not officially immigrated to Israel. Since it was an immersion class, and only Hebrew was spoken, during the breaks we tended to congregate with others who spoke our native language.

During one break, I approached Connie, who was

from Canada. She was not Jewish, but she was living in Israel with her Israeli boyfriend, Daniel.

"I met him at the bottom of a cave spelunking in New Zealand," she told me that first day.

"Spa-whating?" I asked. I had no idea what she was talking about.

"We were both traveling the world, fell in love at the bottom of a cave and decided to make a go of our relationship. So here I am, living in Tel Aviv, trying to learn the language," she said.

She gestured excitedly as she spoke. She had blond curly hair and bright blue eyes. With her tanned skin and athletic build, she looked like a walking advertisement for an outdoor store. I thought her story was cool, and I was excited to finally have a friend.

Another day, during a break, Connie and I started chatting with Alejandra, an 18-year-old from Buenos Aires. She'd made Aliyah to Israel with her sister, leaving their parents behind. Even though I was only a few years older than her, I immediately felt protective of her.

"Was it hard to leave your family?" I asked. My innate curiosity for other people and their personal stories overtook me. "Why did you leave your country? How are you liking Israel so far?"

She answered as best she could in a combination of English, Hebrew and Spanish, and I got the gist of what she was saying. She had traveled to Israel for free and did not bring any personal effects. The country subsidized everything including her health care, food, clothing, housing and even the Ulpan. With tears in her eyes, she shared how hard life had been in Israel and how much she missed her family. She said antisemitism was terrible in her country, and her parents wanted her and her sister to have a better life. The education, jobs and opportunities would be better in Israel. Even though I was there for very different reasons, I understood how she felt. Life in this new place was hard and lonely.

The three of us became friends, and soon an older woman, Anna, from Munich, joined our group. She was a single mother, closer to 40, and she had moved to Israel with her child. I was surprised to learn Jewish people were still living in Munich. Her English was excellent, and her friendliness bubbled over. Any misconceptions I had about all Germans being Nazis fell away because of Anna, with her friendly smile and dimpled left cheek. She had moved to Israel in search of work opportunities and a better life for her daughter.

My world was enriched with my new group of

international friends. I had stories to share in the evenings when Jordan and I would dine on fresh pasta and vegetables on the patio at Marilyn Monroe's with Sonya close by. Jordan was pleased I had something to call my own and we enjoyed sharing stories at the end of our days.

Sometimes, on warm, quiet evenings, after watching "Dawson's Creek"—one of the only TV shows in English that was even slightly appealing, I would write group emails to family and friends back home detailing my experiences, conversations and encounters. Through this writing I felt more connected to my former life in Minneapolis. I received wonderful accounts from my friends about what was going on in their lives, and my mom wrote almost every day. I lived for that lifeline back home. I was starting to feel more comfortable and settled in Israel, and my Hebrew was coming along quickly. I didn't realize what a large vocabulary I had acquired until words would just pop into my brain. The Ulpan was helping tremendously.

My days typically consisted of my Ulpan in the mornings and then my two-hour walk with Sonya in the afternoons. I discovered a fresh juice stand right near the Supersol grocery store. They squeezed juices from plums, peaches, apples, oranges and many other fresh delicious fruits. I craved the juice and became a regular there.

I also picked up running. I had been a runner on and off my entire life, and this seemed like the perfect place to begin again. My runs connected me back to my dad and the long runs we took together when I was growing up. While out running, I noticed signs on light posts all over the city that said "English tutor wanted" and "help wanted" with a phone number listed on multiple tabs along the bottom that could be torn off.

I had tried to get a work permit at the visa office, but after waiting in line for three hours, I was told I could not get one unless an employer sent a letter stating they needed my services. Most companies would not even talk to me without the permit, so it was a catch-22. I would have to do work "illegally" if I wanted any kind of paycheck.

I wasn't sure what kind of job I would get, but I kept an open mind. The Internet was in its infancy in 1997. In my spare time, I went down a rabbit hole on my computer and taught myself the basics of HTML and coding during evenings while Jordan was studying. I created a few of my own signs, starting with "English tutor" and "English editing for your website and business materials." As I hung them around our neighborhood, I pulled many tabs from other signs and started making calls. By now, we had a landline with a local phone number, which made it a lot easier to communicate with people.

Right away, I found a job as an English tutor for a woman named Marianne. She had moved to Israel from Russia, where she was treated poorly because her passport had the word "Jewish" stamped on it. Everywhere she went she ran into trouble for being a Jew.

The first time we met at our apartment, she told me more about her life. "I couldn't even go to the movies," she explained in a quiet, sad voice.

I shuddered, leaning in.

It was hard to reconcile her experience with my large Jewish family and tight-knit Jewish community back home. I had moved around freely, able to attend Jewish camp, bar/bat mitzvahs and holidays and never really thought twice about my religion. Antisemitism was on my radar, not in the ways she was describing, but I knew it still existed, even in the United States. I wanted Marianne to feel the freedom that I felt. I quickly realized how much she gave up to start her new life in Israel. At the time, I couldn't have foreseen a spike in antisemitism in my own country, or that there would be a time when I'd think twice before sharing with someone that I was Jewish.

We sat together on my black futon couch, and I became captivated by Marianne's life. As we practiced her English, I realized how lucky I was to be paid to have conversations with her. I would have done it for free. But she insisted on paying me. As her rich stories spilled out, I learned that she spoke five languages, something I hadn't realized was so common among non-Americans.

"I have tried to get a visa to visit the United States many times," she said with a faraway look in her brown eyes. "My goal is to get to the U.S. and live the American dream."

The American Dream. I played this idea over and over in my head after she left. I thought about how lucky I was to be born in the United States and live a free life. All the people I'd met in Israel were running away from their home countries to start new lives, often leaving behind jobs, homes and family. I had begun to realize that there was a great big world out there I knew little about. The word gratitude wasn't on my radar at this point in my life, but I'm pretty sure I felt something akin to it in that moment.

As time marched on, I became more settled. I got hired for freelance work. For my first job, I worked on a CD-ROM program called, "Unlocking the Bible Codes," which allowed users to search Hebrew scriptures for hidden codes without any knowledge of Hebrew. You'd type the English word you wanted to find, and then the program translated the word to Hebrew automatically, and searched and analyzed the scripture, returning all the hidden messages that contained the word.

I edited all the English copy, helped them set up their website, and helped compose end-user text that explained the program. I enjoyed having the work, but it was a short-lived project. My next job was for a company called Buckeye, which was a flying ATV that was just being introduced in Israel. I helped create marketing materials in English for them.

Much of my freelance work was done from our apartment, so I was able to go to my Ulpan each day and spend time walking Sonya. I started to plan weekend outings in Tel Aviv and around the country.

Sometimes Jordan's med school friends would join us out, and it was often just me and the guys. We would go to The Hard Rock Cafe on Dizengoff Street, a major thoroughfare and commercial shopping area. We'd go to movies on weekends. When "Titanic" was in the theaters there, I took everyone I knew in Israel to see it with me and saw it four times. I loved the passionate, romantic love story and the mere act of going to an American movie in Israel allowed me to feel lost in the moment, in the theater, for a few hours.

Jordan and I also traveled out of the country every three months. We found it was easier to live in Israel on a tourist visa than jumping through all the hoops for him to get annual student visas. All we needed to do was leave the country and return through the passport control at the borders. We were privileged to travel to Egypt, Jordan, Greece, Turkey, Czech Republic and Hungary. I looked forward to each new adventure and started planning the next one almost as soon as we returned.

Our trip to Petra, Jordan, was one I'll never forget. It was a bucket list destination for me after watching "Indiana Jones and the Last Crusade" years earlier. The ancient city of Petra or "Red Rose City" was carved from rose-red sandstone and was the ruins of an ancient metropolis and trading center, hidden in the desert hills. Jordan and I took a four-hour bus ride through the desert to Eilat, a tourist destination city at the bottom tip of Israel where it meets the Red Sea, with the Sinai Peninsula on one side and the country of Jordan on the other. We arrived at the Jordanian border to cross over and to connect with the transfer company that would take us to our youth hostel outside of Petra. As we walked across into Jordan, the hair on my arms stood up. I was nervous, heading into an Arab country that had declared peace with the state of Israel just a few years earlier, following decades of war and enmity. Now, in 1997, relationships were still strained between the Jordanian people and the Israelis, and we could feel the tension in the air even though the borders were open for tourism. We were traveling as Americans and not as Jews, as that seemed to be the safer option at the moment. We knew the ride to Petra was about two hours, mostly traversing the hot desert.

We hopped into our van that was waiting for us. "Brother-sister, right?" the driver said.

"Huh?" I said, confused.

"You are brother, sister," he repeated again, with authority.

"Yes," Jordan answered, nodding his head in agreement and locking eyes with me so I would understand. "She is my sister."

And so, it was settled. We would travel as "siblings" and not as an engaged couple. There would be no hand holding. Jordan would be "in charge" of me for the next 48 hours as we spent two days and one night in this Arab country. I felt uneasy the entire time we were there. But Petra was incredible—the elaborate buildings carved into the mountains, the natural beauty of the surrounding landscape.

Another time we traveled to Eilat in a rented white Kia. We left the car there, walked a few miles to the Egyptian border, and crossed into the Egyptian Sinai Peninsula. The Sinai is the large desert area between Egypt and Israel that belonged to Israel from 1973 to 1982, before it was given back to Egypt in a peace settlement. We took a two-hour cab ride with five other passengers to Dahab, Egypt, where we would spend the night. Our Bedouin driver, dressed in a white cotton robe and head scarf, strapped our luggage to the top of his roof with string. The ride was nerve-wracking, the driver swerving between lanes and turning off his headlights as oncoming cars approached. The drive was stunning, though, and as the road twisted through the mountains, I held on for dear life and prayed we wouldn't have a head-on collision.

As we continued, the Gulf of Aqaba alongside us, the full moon reflected off the water and we could see across the sea to Saudi Arabia. We finally made it to our $28-per-night private room at the "resort" and fell fast asleep. The next day we relaxed on the beach and swam in the clearest and cleanest water

I have ever seen. The Sinai has miles and miles of untouched beaches with nothing else in sight. It was so beautiful that we decided to take it easy and enjoy the beach in preparation for our evening.

We found a cab driver around 11 p.m. who drove us the two hours to the base of Mount Sinai to make the challenging three-mile, two-hour trek up to the top to watch the sun rise. This was the site in the Old Testament where Moses received the Ten Commandments from God. I was more interested in the experience of the climb, the sunrise and the views from the top than the religious aspects of the pilgrimage. The hike up was freezing, but invigorating and beautiful. I had never in my life seen stars so clear and bright, and our path was lit by the night sky. I even saw a shooting star. There were thousands of steps, and it was one of the most challenging hikes I had done in my life.

At the top we rented three blankets and a mat, bought some hot chocolate from a Bedouin tent, and camped out on a rock as we waited for the sun to rise. It was so cold as we huddled together and waited and waited as more and more people ascended. By the time the sun started to light up the sky, there were mobs of people singing. It was total craziness. We joined in for "Hatikvah"—the Israeli national anthem. The sheer beauty was magnificent. I took in where I was and what I was doing at that very moment, realizing I would most likely never be there again.

Once the sun had risen completely, we were anxious to go back down. We took a more difficult trail this time, which was a big mistake. I twisted my ankle several times, and by the time we reached the bottom hours later, it was the size of an elephant's. Both Jordan and I were physically exhausted from being up all night and from the hike and we crashed in the taxi back to Dahab.

The next day, as we made it back to the Israeli border, we were unable to catch a cab to take us back to our rental car. My ankle was in rough shape, and I didn't think I could walk the few miles to our car.

"Jordan," I said in pain as I attempted to bear my full weight on my ankle. "What are we going to do? I'm not sure how much farther I can walk." We were carrying all our luggage on our backs and scorching in the hot sun. Sweat dripped down my back.

We continued walking for another hour. I was exhausted and angry with Jordan. I was dreaming of a cold swimming pool, or taking a dip in the gleaming Red Sea, which we could see in the distance.

"What if I leave you here with our bags and go get the car?"

"I guess," I answered, not actually feeling comfortable being left alone on the side of the road near the border but trying to contain the frustration bubbling inside me. I didn't think I had another choice. I watched carloads of people drive past and attempted to hitchhike, but no one stopped. So I focused on how far I'd come, how different I was from that scared girl in Boston with her mother. I was halfway around the world, and I was managing on my own. Before I knew it, Jordan appeared with the car.

Sometimes on the weekends, I would join my distant cousins Noa and Moshe and their two small children, Hadas and Nir, on a local hiking adventure, and I felt the sense of belonging and family I had missed since moving to Israel. We would pile into their army green, mud-covered SUV and zip off-road to beautiful places I would have never found on my own.

Once we drove up into the North on Mount Gilboa, a beautiful, forested area that reminded me of San Francisco. Three-quarters of the way up the mountain, in the middle of nowhere, we stopped at a restaurant called Gilboa Herb Farm. It was a true farm-to-table experience, well before the term was known. The tiny restaurant grew and raised much of the food it served—vegetables, spices, medicinal herbs, chickens. We sat at a picnic table on an alpine wooden terrace with views of the Gilboa Valley, the mountains of Nazareth, Caramel, Mount Tabor and even Mount Hermon, and we were served the most delicious food I had tasted since arriving in Israel. And I loved the food in Israel. Everything was super healthy and fresh, whether it was from a fancy restaurant or a simple seaside cafe.

My cousins talked a lot about life in Israel and shared their perspectives on the difficult political conflicts that hung like an ugly cloud over day-to-day life.

"It's complicated," explained my cousin Noa. "There are the Orthodox and the secular Jews, Druze, the Bedouins, and the Palestinians. We must figure out how we can all live together in peace and harmony."

There was also the threat of Sadam Hussein and the war with Iraq. Jordan and I registered with the U.S. embassy, bought gas masks when the threat of anthrax and biological weapons increased, and regularly made evacuation plans. My mom wanted me to come home, but Jordan couldn't leave school, and the news stories made everything seem worse than it actually felt. Life went on in Israel. People went to work, school, out to dinner—but there was tension in the air and a state of alertness everywhere. At the mall down the street from our apartment, armed Zahal (Israeli army) guards with M-16s checked bags at the door for bombs. This was standard procedure in Israel. I felt safe with the Zahal officers guarding the public spaces, and I tried not to think about how close in age we were.

My cousins began to include us more in their lives. We were invited to Hadas' Bedouin birthday party. A Bedouin man came with a tent and made fresh, delicious, warm pita on an open fire, prepared tea and told the children stories. The kids sat around him, enthralled.

Finally, instead of calling home in tears, I had many exciting stories to share. I continued to write weekly emails detailing my experiences and received wonderful responses back from friends: "I love hearing about your adventures!" "You are so lucky to be having this experience!" "I have always wanted to live in another country!" "I can't believe all the cool places you are visiting!" Sometimes, I'd feel a pang of sadness about what I was missing back home, but I had also grown to love my new city.

I didn't realize how much I had stretched myself until Jordan pointed it out one day.

"I think you finally lean on me more than on your parents. It's nice that you're not calling them for every little thing anymore or asking them for their opinions."

"I guess it took me moving across the world to finally cut the cord," I laughed, thrilled with the discovery. I had sensed a change in myself, and I was happy Jordan noticed it too. I felt content that we were becoming "us" without the influences of our parents, especially mine. I was inhabiting my own self away from my family of origin and becoming self-reliant.

That summer we came home to get married and celebrate, surrounded by family and friends. We brought Sonya home knowing she would not return with us. Large, golf ball-sized lumps had formed all over her body, and with her older age, it was clear she was living on borrowed time.

My parents were overjoyed to see her, and she seemed surprised and delighted to be back. Tears welled in my dad's eyes as he said quietly, "Hi pup. Welcome home."

"She had a great life in Tel Aviv," I told my dad. "She loved it there—the sights, the smells, the walks, the beach—all of it. We spent more time together than we ever would have back home." My face was wet with tears. "I'm so glad she came. I needed her and she needed me. We helped each other through."

Sonya died peacefully in my arms a few days after we returned home. I remember the loss like it was yesterday. I could sense her around me for months after she died, could feel her calming presence. I knew I would not have another dog for a long time. Losing Sonya was painful.

Our wedding ended up being a wonderful distraction. I felt like a fairy princess in the most beautiful and elegant setting complete with stunning flowers, ice sculptures, a gorgeous cake and a fabulous band. We danced all night. I felt so happy to be surrounded by the comfort and warmth of our friends and families that part of me did not want to leave again. But I was also excited to return to Israel.

After the wedding, we had a short honeymoon in Cabo San Lucas (we opted to stay closer to home) and headed back to Tel Aviv for Jordan's third year of medical school a few weeks later.

The move back was much easier. I missed Sonya desperately, but I occupied my time with project-based work and adventures with friends I'd made there.

On Thursdays, we drove to Nachalot Binyamin and "the shuk," an open-air market and weekly art fair. It took place on a cobblestone street where no cars were allowed. All kinds of artists hosted small booths filled with handmade jewelry, paintings, Judaica, toys and crafts. It was a great spot to buy gifts and roam around. Around the corner was the shuk, an outdoor market that was like Costco, Target and a hardware store all in one. There were rows and rows of booths, and you could buy literally anything. Stacked high were bright-colored fruits and vegetables, and the spices in rich oranges, yellows and browns. And there were the sounds of shoppers bargaining all around.

"I'll give you 20 shekels!" one young woman yelled at a shop owner.

"No, 25 shekels!" the shop owner countered firmly.

Bargaining in the Middle East was like a pastime. It would be considered foolish to purchase anything without haggling for a lower price, the clear mark of a foreigner.

And the smells? The scents of challahs and barekkahs and chocolate croissants wafted all around. It was an outing I enjoyed immensely.

In 1999, during Jordan's fourth year of med school,

we moved back to the United States to give him a few months to work in U.S. hospitals on rotations and to interview for residency positions. Life would become much busier and more complicated. I would cherish the memories of our time in Israel, just the two of us exploring the country and the world together. By summer, Jordan start-ed residency at the University of Minnesota Hospital, and I was pregnant with our first baby. Moving to Israel was my "growing up" experience where Jordan and I became a family.

CHAPTER FOUR

**The thing that is really hard, and really amazing, is giving up being perfect, and beginning the work of becoming yourself.
—ANNA QUINDLEN**

I first stepped onto my yoga mat about two months after my first child, Zach, was born. I had been experiencing significant back pain, and someone suggested I try Bikram yoga to sweat off the baby weight. My doctor said it might help. I understood the physical health benefits, but I had no idea the impact yoga would have in helping me develop my voice and find my way to my true self.

Zach came into the world with large brown eyes and sandy brown hair. An old soul, a deep thinker. At 2 days old, he was studying me and Jordan intensely with a furrowed brow and the look of an old man. I imagined him thinking, "Who are these people? Why am I here?"

At about a week old he seemed to wake up, and his screaming and crying set in—as did my back pain. I was exhausted. Jordan was exhausted as well. He was working 36-hour overnight shifts at the hospital every fourth night, which meant I was alone with our now sour-faced, shrieking baby. I was coerced into breastfeeding by everyone around me. Oh, the pain! The bloody nipples, the thrush, and that damn pumping machine. I felt like a cow getting the life squeezed out of me—swish, swish, swish. The sound of that machine, the smell of dried milk, the feeling of engorged breasts—I would never forget it. I spent many days in a white chenille robe that was supposed to be a luxurious new mom gift. Instead, it became the representation of feeling trapped and alone. During those months of early motherhood, I desperately missed the carefree days and warm evenings living in Israel.

As my new mom friends marveled at their perfect babies, I cried and wondered what I did wrong. Why did my baby boy scream? It must be something I was doing wrong, my lactation consultant mother-in-law insisted. Of course, it was all my fault.

"No pacifiers, no bottles, no cribs, only skin to skin contact," my mother-in-law commanded. "And if he is still screaming, you better start to look at your diet."

At the time, I knew little about nutrition and how what I ate could affect my baby. I felt beaten down and like a failure. I envied my bottle-feeding friends with their perfect babies. Why did it have to be so hard?

Some days all I wanted was to take a shower. I would call my mom crying, begging her to come over and hold Zach so I could have 10 precious minutes to myself. She would come running to help, dressed in the latest fashions and part of a world from which I felt so far away. She remained calm and comfortable with Zach, even while he wailed.

Somewhere around 4 months old, Zach stopped screaming. My dad discovered Zach liked to be "bee-bopped," which consisted of a bouncy dance and song: "Bee-bop, bee-bop baby, bee-bop you make me crazy, bee-bop, you're my bee-bop baby boy!" We all sang and bounced Zach over and over again. He laughed and smiled and absolutely loved to be bee-bopped. I was still exhausted, but I did not care. My boy was smiling. We turned a corner, and let me tell you it was a marvelous one.

Zach discovered books and puzzles at a young age. He'd sit on the floor studying and placing the shapes with his chubby little hands until they fit perfectly. He became my pride and joy, and we would sit together in the big rocker in his room and read books together for hours. He had a long attention span for his age.

Still, my insecurities loomed just beneath the surface. I constantly questioned if I was a good mother and compared myself and my baby to others. I took Zach to the doctor when he was 12 months old, worried that he was not talking like other young kids his age. By the time we went back at 18 months, he was speaking in full coherent sentences, and I knew that he was just fine.

"I guess we don't need to worry about that," the young pediatrician said.

It was difficult to find someone to watch Zach and to get myself to a yoga class, but I did it because I needed the respite. Each time, I felt incredibly guilty leaving him. Even thought it was just a few hours, I felt this pull in my chest, like a piece of me was missing.

My days were long and when Jordan came home, exhausted himself, I practically threw Zach at him. I needed a break, and I resented that he got to be out all day while I hadn't gone anywhere. I thought I wanted to stay home and take care of Zach, and I also felt it was expected of me. It was a luxury and I knew I should be grateful, but it was damn hard work. Sometimes I envied the moms who got dressed up, dropped their babies at daycare and went off to their office jobs downtown. But I knew that juggling act would get old after about a week.

I also knew I needed more. I needed to use my brain. It was crying out to be challenged. One day I mentioned this to my friend, Amy, and she said, "Why don't you try selling promotional products like caps, mugs and pens with logos imprinted on them? It's commission-based work and you can do it on your own schedule. I'm doing it and it's perfect."

"That sounds amazing!" I said, perking up.

I contacted Amy's boss and learned the ropes of the job quickly. I called everyone I knew and told them what I was doing, and soon orders started rolling in. I enjoyed the work. I was essentially a liaison between the customer and the manufacturer, handling all the details for the customer. But something began to gnaw at me: My boss made a 60 percent profit on each sale I made. She fronted the money to purchase the products, but I did all the work.

After about six months on the job, my dad approached me. "Marnie, why don't you start your own business? I can help you get an LLC set up," he said. "Then you can keep all of your profits."

Once again, my dad was believing in me and giving me encouragement. He was a self-made serial entrepreneur, so it came naturally to him to think outside the box and dream big. I'm not sure why I hadn't considered it sooner, maybe because I was pregnant again and focusing on getting enough rest. But I loved the idea and was jazzed about it almost immediately. I didn't need to think on it; I was in.

A couple of weeks later, once I decided on a name, registered my limited liability corporation, and started to get organized, I let my boss know. I was worried that she'd be upset that I was starting a business exactly like hers. Surprisingly, she wasn't. She had done the same thing herself many years earlier. She encouraged me to become registered as a woman-owned business. And that is how ChillyBean Promotions, named after Zach, my little chilly bean, was born.

Our daughter Sage was born a few months later, and I was relieved that she was a super mellow baby. She had gorgeous almond-shaped brown eyes, thick dark lashes and beautiful olive skin. She was petite from day one—everything about her was dainty. We chose the name Sage because it was unique, and because it held a double meaning—representing both wisdom and an earthy spice.

Sage was born with a red spot on her forehead and upper lip, which I learned was called a nevus flammeus. I took her to a dermatologist who explained they were just superficial blood vessels. She would outgrow them; by the time she was in middle school and later an adult, you could probably only see them if she got angry or exerted herself. I worried so much about the marks. As she grew monthly, they became fainter and fainter. But people stopped me all the time to ask what they were. I was defensive because I didn't like how others focused on my little girl's appearance. She did eventually outgrow them.

Sage slept on my chest for her first six months of life. Her small head cradled in the nape of my neck. I loved and hated this. I don't think I slept soundly that entire time for fear she would roll off and fall on the floor. Or worse, I would roll over her and crush her. Though we hadn't with Zach, we gave her a pacifier or "ba" as she called it later, for self-soothing. We were much more relaxed as second-time parents, and I found myself enjoying motherhood much more.

Zach had grown into a happy preschooler. He quickly figured out how to navigate the world around him, intensely curious about how things worked. He questioned everything, his brain a giant sponge. He became my teacher on a daily basis, showing me new ways to see and experience the world. He would ask big questions, like what happens after death, where babies came from, and how the universe worked.

I enjoyed our conversations immensely, and they continued throughout his childhood. To this day, discussions with him make me dig in and think deeply about various topics. He is truly an old soul—I still wonder how many other lives he lived and touched before he entered this one.

Life was busy. I was running my small business, taking care of two kids, plus managing everything at home—finances, grocery shopping, household tasks, social plans, travel, kid appointments, you name it. While Jordan worked, I kept our lives running smoothly. Most of the time I didn't mind, but sometimes it was exhausting. I just wanted to be taken care of, something that would come up repeatedly in our relationship.

"Maybe you could plan something for us to do Saturday night," I would say, dropping the hint instead of being direct about what I wanted or needed.

"Want to play tennis?" he would say. Tennis? Didn't he understand I wanted to be taken out for a nice, relaxing, kid-free dinner?

"That wasn't exactly what I had in mind," I'd retort, crossing my arms against my chest. "Never mind, I will figure something out for us." And it often ended there.

Sometimes I would complain about this to my

mom and she would say, "He is exactly like your father." Not really what I wanted to hear, either.

Yoga was the space where I could focus on myself.

I would meet my friend Nicole, who had two little ones the same ages as Zach and Sage, for yoga class. She would show up with her designer yoga bag looking way more put together than I looked or felt. I immediately fell in love with the physical practice of yoga. I loved the feeling of power and strength in the strong standing poses like warrior two and tree pose. And the vulnerability I felt on the floor in pigeon pose and plow. I had always enjoyed movement and dance, even with my naturally tight hamstrings. I relished stepping into the studio as if it were an alternate reality, being greeted by the owner, Mary, who was also the teacher. She was 15 or so years older than me, and her brown eyes crinkled in the corners when she smiled. She had a peacefulness about her that drew me into the present the moment I entered the small studio, which smelled of heat, sweat and melted candles.

"How are you today, Marnie?" Mary would ask as I slipped off my light brown Uggs and stripped down to my black leggings and tank top. I was often one of the last students to arrive. I would answer with a quick, "Good, thanks," as I quietly entered the room, laid on the mat, and waited for class to begin. There was no chatter, which I would later learn was not the case at other yoga studios. I welcomed the silence and the precious moments on my back in savasana or corpse pose. I think I unconsciously understood the healing power of lying on the floor, letting my chest rise and fall in a slow, uncontrolled, rhythmic breath. I was drawn back to this tiny unknown gem of a studio over and over again. My body seemed to know it needed the rest.

After many months of attending Bikram yoga, Nicole and I moved on to Ashtanga, a type of yoga based on eight principles. It consists of a series of poses executed in swift succession, combined with deep, controlled breathing. We followed a guru, Jill, to a local big box gym where I learned about alignment, proper posture, and how to use my breath properly.

"Breathe in four counts, hold your breath at the top and breathe out four counts," she would say in a quiet, soothing voice. She had an air about her and seemed to float around the room. She was a mere 5 feet tall, but she commanded respect. I knew not to mess with her, and everyone else in the room did too.

Breathing seemed so basic, yet I had to train my

body to breathe properly. All my life I had gulped in air with my abdominal muscles tense and never relaxed into my breathing. I think it caused my energy to become stuck in my chest cavity and along my spine. When I was in elementary school, maybe second grade, the school nurse performed scoliosis checks on all the kids. We lined up in the hallway by grade, waiting our turn to bend forward as she slid her hands up and down our spines to check for an S-curve or a C-curve. Kids who were deemed OK were sent back to class. Kids who weren't had to report to the nurse's office. I was the only one who got sent to the nurse's office. I was embarrassed to be singled out and worried I might need to wear a metal brace to keep my back straight. I was a gymnast—how would it affect that? Why did I have to be different? Why was my body letting me down?

My mom took me to an orthopedic doctor later that week. He concurred that I did have a mild C-curve, but that I wouldn't need any treatment, just some exercises I could do at home on my own. I began obsessing over my back from that point forward. I would never have the perfect and flat back that I longed for. I would always have the curve like a chimpanzee, I thought to myself.

But I had found Jill, and she was a stickler about

alignment. She would glide around the class making adjustments to everyone's posture. She taught me so much about how to move my body safely. She didn't view me as different and taught me how to work with the body I had. She made accommodations for every posture, and I appreciated the relief I felt from my back pain.

**May your choices reflect your hopes,
not your fears.
—NELSON MANDELA**

There was life before the accident, and life after.

Before the accident, despite my dad's earlier addiction, part of me still clung to the idea of "my perfect family." This extended beyond my large Dachis family and into the little family of four Jordan and I had created. I had my boy, Zach, and my new baby daughter, Sage.

On December 21, 2003, my perfect world came crashing down. I was vacationing (as much as one can vacation with a 3-month-old baby and a 3-year-old) in Palm Springs, California, with my parents, my brother and his then wife and their young children. I brought our high school-aged babysitter along for an extra set of hands, because as chief resident, Jordan had to stay home. To my disappointment, he had to work long hours in the hospital over the Christmas holiday.

On that sunny, warm December day, my beautiful

and innocent 16-month-old nephew somehow toddled his way outside alone and fell into the swimming pool. On Christmas Day, after four excruciating days of waiting at Loma Linda Hospital, he died. Years later, I still can't wrap my mind around it, even as the truth and loss stare back at me from the page.

It felt like we were all living in a nightmare, and at any moment we would wake up. We would be sitting around the large dining table, laughing and talking, eating delicious food, the kids playing at our feet, my baby wrapped tightly in my arms.

Three-year-old Zach didn't understand what was happening as we sat on the cold, hard floor of the hospital, our backs pressed against the concrete wall, waiting, waiting and waiting. Eventually he vomited all over that pristine floor, the smell so pungent it made me gag. It was too much. I gulped for air. I was suffocating. I played the events over in my mind and then forced them away, hoping to wake up from the nightmare. Christmas decor was all around— shiny green and red garland lined the walls, and Bing Crosby's "Silver Bells" and "I'll Be Home for Christmas" played in the hallways. I wanted to vomit like Zach.

After we lost my nephew, everyone in my family collapsed into their own worlds. It was difficult to communicate with one another. Our traumatized sitter, who had been helping me with my kids inside the house at the time of the accident, flew back home the day of the accident. She was still a child herself, and not quite able to process what had happened. Jordan took an emergency leave of absence from work and flew to Palm Springs to be with family and help us get home.

Back in Minnesota, we were in a fog. We went through the motions of everyday tasks like showering, taking care of the kids, grocery shopping, making dinner and so on, but we weren't present for any of it. The news about my nephew and his funeral and shiva (period of Jewish mourning) flew through our small community, and my phone rang off the hook. I couldn't bear to speak to anyone about it. I found it a relief when I was among strangers. I would introduce myself as Marnie Marmet, rather than Marnie Dachis, in case they had heard about my nephew. I was living in a heightened state where I felt like I was fleeing from a wild animal that was chasing me. My body would shake, and my heart would race. Everyone wanted details about the accident, and no one knew exactly what to say. It was too horrible for words. I felt like people were staring at me everywhere I went and like I could burst into tears at any moment. I held my babies close to me constantly. I only wanted to breathe in their clean scents, smother myself into their innocence. I would not let them out of my sight. I later learned that I was experiencing post-traumatic stress disorder (PTSD).

I sometimes panicked when I was away from my kids. I didn't want to leave them for anything. The bathtub scared me. I begged Jordan to upgrade our home security system. We installed alarms on all our bedroom windows, even though they were on the second story, because I was terrified someone would steal our children in the middle of the night. I knew this was irrational, but I couldn't talk myself out of it. The avalanche of those horrible memories haunted me. My mind kept hitting replay, and all I wanted was for my nephew to be back, alive, safe. I couldn't sleep at night; I worried about the what-ifs. How would I ever be apart from my children again?

When summer rolled around, we had to deal with the pool in our own backyard. I hated it. I couldn't look at it without thinking about drowning. I constantly worried about my kids falling in. We hired someone to install an ugly black mesh interlocking fence around the pool. The locked gate into the pool area was so hard to open that I couldn't do it while holding Sage tightly in my arms. We activated an annoying high-pitched alarm that sounded each time an exterior door opened.

My next step was swimming lessons for Zach. I knew this was extremely important, but I had white-knuckle anxiety around the water. Before, my love for the water ran deep. I had grown up spending summers boating on Lake Minnetonka and swimming, water-skiing and canoeing at sleep-away camp. I spent hours swimming and lounging with friends in our own backyard pool. I loved visiting and swimming and snorkeling in the ocean as well. The sound of the water methodically lapping up on the shore and the wonderful smell of salt and fresh air together was soothing. The water was a place for me to unwind and relax. That was before.

After, water took my breath away.

I didn't like the nervous wreck I had become. I found a hippie therapist who saw patients in her home and drove 10 minutes to see her once a week. We sat in her living room, with her piano and tchotchkes. Sometimes her teenage daughter would walk through the front door and pass by during our sessions. I never felt fully at ease, but it was all I could muster at the time. I needed tools. I needed to vent to someone other than Jordan. I needed to rehash things, to make sense of something nonsensical. I was confused.

I didn't know where to seek comfort for my pain. Everyone in my entire family was soaking in their own pain.

Although I was Jewish and considered myself culturally and spiritually connected to my religion, I had never been particularly religious. I often questioned the existence of God in my mind, but I was drawn to the beautiful music, traditional foods, family customs and supportive community as sources of comfort in my religion. After my nephew's accident I was certain there was no God. I did not believe it anymore. No all-powerful presence would take such an innocent soul. I was astounded by the number of times people said to me, "This was God's will," or "For some reason this was meant to happen," or "He is in a better place now."

Well, fuck you. I couldn't agree less. I would plaster a fake smile on my face and nod or smile meekly, not having the energy or the words to disagree.

Someone suggested that I read the book "Many Lives, Many Masters: The True Story of a Psychiatrist, His Young Patient and Past-Life Therapy" by Dr. Brian Weiss. And so I did. This book resonated with me. It gave me hope that there was something after death and that reincarnation could be possible. That

I would meet my loved ones again somewhere in space and time. I had always believed in something out there in the universe; I wasn't quite sure what "it" was, but I knew it was not an all-powerful God looking down on me.

I stayed in therapy for about six months. It was where I first started to learn and understand PTSD. We talked through all kinds of scenarios in which I could move forward in my life without so much fear of death and accidents. But the fears continued to grip me. I didn't consider myself to be an overbearing, overprotective parent before the accident, and I did not like who I had become since: hovering, having trouble leaving my kids with anyone else. When our babysitter would come, I'd leave a list of all the things to do in an emergency. I made sure all our sitters were CPR and first-aid certified. I left the phone numbers for poison control and our emergency contacts in case something happened. I made them text me regularly with updates.

I had to actively remind myself that my family of four was alive and healthy and safe. I felt guilty about this. Why was I so lucky? I gained a deeper understanding of gratitude, even if it was tinged with guilt. I felt tremendous relief each time I looked into my beautiful children's faces. I still feel this way today when I see them.

On top of my own pain and stress, both my parents sank into a deep depression. I'd never seen them so down in my entire life. Dark hollow eyes, no laughter, no will to engage in much of anything. Even time with their living grandchildren did not bring them joy. It became difficult to be around them. Being together was a constant reminder of the accident. We had been through so much together, but it was easier to keep a bit of physical distance. I still spoke to my mom daily on the phone, but I started to rely on the support of friends more than my mom.

Some friends became like family during this time, checking in by phone daily, planning outings with the kids and couples' dinners without the kids. They understood that I did not want to talk about the accident and protected me.

Small moments helped lift the darkness: Zach would sing a funny song or say something silly. Sage would share her first smiles and giggles, have her first bites of peas—all the milestones that came with her first year of life.

But my parents' depression distressed me. I began to make it my mission to help them find joy in life again. I didn't realize yet that I couldn't do this for them, that they would need to find their way back to happiness on their own. It also didn't cross my mind that this would not be the only low moment they would hit in my lifetime.

Six years after the accident, I still felt fearful around water. I decided to challenge myself by signing up for a triathlon. It was a huge undertaking and included open-water swim practice. My training started in a pool, and I soon moved to a large lake. I worked with a swim coach who helped me learn to breathe, to stroke efficiently, and to increase my overall comfort in the water. I had several panic attacks during the lessons and would jerk my head out of the water, gasping for air. But I was determined to work through my fear.

The day of the triathlon was nerve-racking. Swimming was the first part of the race, and I was thankful for it. But I quickly discovered I did not like being surrounded by flapping arms and legs, so I took my sweet time. I completed that first triathlon and went on to do one more. Then I hung up my swim cap and vowed never to swim in crowded waters again.

**Everyone is my teacher. Some I seek.
Some I subconsciously attract.
Often I learn simply by observing others.
—ERIC ALLEN**

I continued to turn to yoga as I grieved as a way to heal and connect with my breath. By the time Gabi, my younger daughter, came along, a small yoga studio had opened near our house. I made the switch to that studio and Vinyasa yoga, which moves from one pose directly into the next. There's a flow to a Vinyasa yoga session, though the specific poses, and the pace varies from one instructor to the next. I loved this faster-paced yoga practice set to whatever music the teacher of the moment chose. This studio had mirrors on the walls, and my eyes darted around the room to look at other students. Was I doing the pose better or worse than the person next to me? Why wasn't the teacher praising me in class or coming to correct my alignment? Or better yet, giving me a massage in savasana at the end of the practice? I still hadn't shaken my habit of comparing myself to others or caring too much about what others thought of me.

Yet I loved the studio and the way my body felt after each practice—the "yoga high"—as I floated out of the studio and back to my chaotic home. With three small children and Jordan working nonstop, my life continued to be full.

Everybody loved Gabi, the baby of the family. She had big brown eyes and the cutest dimple when she smiled. Her eyes danced all the time. Her ears stuck out a bit like mine, but somehow, they looked gorgeous on her. Since I was a little girl, I was told I had the "Benowitz ears" like my grandmother and mother. This was not a good thing. It meant my ears stuck out like Dumbo, were too large for my head, stuck on to my face like a Mr. Potato Head. I was never told my ears made me unique or beautiful. My ears didn't fit.

I dreamt of wearing casual ponytails or a single braid down my back, but when I tried it and looked in the mirror, all I saw were my clunky ears. It was my internal voice gnawing at me, finding faults in myself. I noticed everyone's perfectly delicate ears. I wondered what my face would look like with my ears pinned back. Would I still look like me?

Still, a part of me liked my ears. They were all mine. Hidden under my hair, beneath baseball caps, tucked in tight like a child snug in their bed. The utility of my ears has truly been a blessing. Listening has been magnificent. Enjoying music has been magical. Their purpose alone has been instrumental in my daily happiness. And seeing the Benowitz ears passed down to another generation, my younger daughter, I could see only their beauty.

Gabi was the happiest baby ever. And so independent. When she was tired as a toddler, she would crawl up the stairs on her own and lie on the floor in her bedroom until we put her in her crib. She worshiped her brother, then age 7, and sister, age 4, and was schlepped (dragged along) to every activity under the sun.

The good news was that she had no problem napping on the go. She smiled at each person she met. Gabi realized at a young age that if she was funny, she had everyone's attention. Making people laugh became routine for her; she would make us all laugh daily. "It's the Gabi show, oh yeah!" she would sing in her adorable, high-pitched voice. She sounded like a cartoon character.

I loved my three kids, and spending time with them, but it was a lot of work. When Jordan was home, we worked alongside one another making simple dinners, doing laundry and other tasks around the house. He was helpful. But he worked a lot, and time was always a negotiation with Jordan. I was constantly bartering for a vacation and time away from our kids. I needed breaks, but he didn't seem to. He had no problem being sleep-deprived or living a life with just work and home with nothing in between. He felt fulfilled.

I needed more. In addition to work and family time, I needed time with girlfriends, time out of the house, time to go out as adults. Jordan and I didn't always see eye-to-eye, and I was often resentful during those years. I complained and demanded a lot. And I also felt a lot of guilt because he was working so hard.

A college-aged sitter came to our house so I could attend yoga classes several times per week. I reverently looked up to my teachers, the way I used to look up to my camp counselors as a kid. They wove detailed stories of their lives into their classes, and I immersed myself in the safe community they created. I found myself thinking of them when I was home; I admired so many of them. I dreamed of having the poise and confidence to lead a class of my own someday.

When my kids were 9, 6 and 3, my friend Nicole and I decided to go on a yoga retreat in Tulum, Mexico. At the time, Tulum was an off-the-beaten-path beach bum town, two hours south of Cancun by shuttle. The free-spirited teachers leading the retreat both hailed from our city, but they were from another yoga studio. Aside from each other, Nicole and I did not know anyone else at the retreat. We were both so ready to have a break from our little ones and focus on ourselves that we could barely contain our excitement. It took a great deal of planning and help from our families to leave our children behind and make it happen.

When we got to the airport, Nicole's suitcase weighed 75 pounds—25 pounds over the limit. Her bag felt like she had filled it with stones! My own bag was bigger in size but was somehow much lighter than hers.

I imagined white sand, the blue ocean, an array of fresh, healthy, colorful foods, beautiful accommodations right on the beach where we would relax, unwind and practice a little yoga.

After a long and bumpy shuttle ride, we arrived at Amansala, which meant peaceful waters. We were shocked to discover the entire resort was on the sand. The buildings were huts and our accommodations were "eco chic." We had no idea what that meant, but we soon found out: no electricity after hours, no locks on the doors of the huts, no glass on the windows, and limited warm water. Inside our hut were two twin beds surrounded with giant bug nets, which we would need to tuck around us to keep the insects out while we slept. The hut was literally on the shore of the turquoise ocean. The view was breathtaking. But we didn't feel particularly safe. People walked freely up and down the beach. At any given moment, a stranger could come into our hut. I imagined someone storming in and kidnapping us in the middle of the night. But I pushed my thoughts aside.

We had both packed hairdryers, flat irons, cute yoga clothes, sundresses and a smattering of other items that we thought were necessities but that we clearly would not need. Maybe I wouldn't even wash my hair!

The great thing about Nicole (who happens to be one of my closest friends and my fashion and beauty advisor) is that she and I travel well together. We can be fiercely independent. We can have our chatty moments, and also sit in total silence with no discomfort. We always manage to have a great time together, with lots of laughs and deep conversation. And we both like to meet new people and hear their stories.

For this trip, I had imagined Nicole sleeping

late and lying on a beach all day. I had imagined I would head out early for yoga or a swim, do some journaling, and then a bit of surfing. By this point I had begun to conquer my fear of the water and had once again found solace in it.

Nicole and I sat in our shanty discussing what to do next, while swatting at ruthless mosquitoes. We decided to leave and find a nicer resort.

We stepped barefoot onto the warm sand and headed down the beach to find Nancy and Ty, the retreat leaders. We found Nancy first, tanned and relaxed in a bikini top and flowing skirt, a headband barely containing her bleached-blond hair. She reminded me of a '70s hippie and emitted a vibe that I liked immediately.

"Hi," I said, clearing my throat. "I think we made a mistake when we signed up for this trip. I'm not sure either of us is cut out for this. We thought the accommodations would be … um … nicer," I said, feeling like a spoiled brat and an idiot at the same time.

But Nancy didn't treat us like we were either of those. She just said, "Please stay for our opening yoga class and dinner. You guys will love it here, I promise."

We felt stuck, and a yoga class and food sounded

appealing. The blazing sun was starting to drop quickly, and we didn't have a solid plan on where we would go, let alone how we would make it all happen.

"Give it a chance," Nancy said in her nurturing voice. "You must be tired from a long, hot travel day." She reminded me of Olivia Newton-John in the movie "Xanadu."

As I lay on my back in savasana and listened to the lull of the ocean, Ty's yoga class had an unbelievable calming effect on me. It may have been that we were in a hut on stilts that overlooked the ocean on all sides. Or the lack of electricity. Or the beautiful hardwood floors that smelled like the beach. Or the fact that we were in a totally new environment surrounded by total strangers. Or a combination of all of those things. But I got completely swept up in the moment.

After class, we floated in the dark to the main hut with a dining area that overlooked the water. It was a cozy, intimate space filled with wooden community tables. Our group of 15 was the only group on the small property. Two drop-dead gorgeous guys in their late 20s or early 30s seemed to appear out of nowhere and described the property, the history, the rules, and how they came to this beach existence. Nicole and I hung on their every word, and as I looked around the room, I realized we were not the only ones captivated by them.

The smell of delicious food wafted from the kitchen and eventually made it to our family-style table. The guacamole was out of this world, and the fresh vegetables and dishes were divine. As we ate, we introduced ourselves. Many of the people appeared interested in bonding and sharing stories of divorce and loss. While I loved meeting new people, I was not interested in engaging in those kinds of conversations. I had specific goals for this trip. I wanted total relaxation, a deeper understanding of yoga and meditation, time to catch up on sleep, a chance to get lost in my thoughts and a good book. And of course, I wanted to enjoy the beautiful surroundings in the sun. I was on this trip because I felt off track at home. I needed some serious self-care. I needed to find myself again.

After dinner, we fumbled back to our hut with only the light of the stars to guide us. I regretted not packing a flashlight. Bugs swarmed around and I started to itch everywhere. All I wanted was to jump inside my bug net and go to sleep. As we opened the door to our hut, a musty smell wafted out. The moonlight reflecting on the water filtered through our front window, but we still couldn't see a thing. We had noticed candles around the room earlier and realized we needed to light them to see. Only we couldn't see anything with which to light them. We remembered one of the men with sculpted arms had mentioned each room had a bell we could ring if there was a problem. We started ringing the bell. It was eerily silent across the property—except for our ruckus—and we felt bad for disrupting the other retreat attendees. Finally, the blue-eyed man showed up.

"Would you mind lighting our candles?" I asked, slightly embarrassed that no one else seemed to be having any issues. The song "Will You Light My Candle?" from the musical "Rent" played in my head.

We chatted easily as he pointed out the igniter and lit the candles. We asked about electricity and hot water, and he explained there were specific hours for taking warm showers because they used solar heaters. He said a couple of the outlets would work during those hours as well, for cell phone charging.

"But no hairdryers!" he exclaimed. "They blow out our system."

Bummer, I thought, wondering if he mentioned that to everyone or just us in particular.

"What's the deal with all the bugs?" I asked. "I'm getting eaten alive here."

"You'll get used to it. This is life on the beach," he said. He seemed to have no bites on his body and was clearly not affected by the bugs.

We got settled. As I crawled into my bug net, I felt exhausted. And I was still a bit spooked. A swatch of fabric barely covered our window, and periodically we heard the voices of people walking on the beach. Our hut was not elevated like some of the others, and we were literally steps from the ocean. It was magnificent, really. I wish I could have appreciated it more that first night. Nicole and I chatted until my eyes closed and I drifted off into sleep.

"NOOO!" I screamed, startling myself awake. A bald man in a long trench coat loomed over me. Where was I?

"Marnie, what's wrong?" Nicole asked, jolting up in her bed. "Are you OK?"

I felt suffocated by the bug net. "I don't know," I murmured, rubbing my eyes in confusion. "There was a man standing over me and it really freaked me out."

I realized I must have sounded crazy. Clearly, I'd had a bad dream.

No one came to check on us that night except

for the adorable golden retrievers that roamed the property. I slept poorly and was up with the sun at 5:30 a.m. As I looked outside, a sense of peace and calm washed over me. But after that rough first night, I knew our sleeping situation would have to change. I stared at the serene ocean and thought about what the Dalai Lama said: "If you think you are too small to make a difference, try sleeping with a mosquito." Then I proceeded to violently scratch and dig at the bites all over my body.

As Nicole and I stumbled half-awake to the yoga hut for the morning class, we discussed how we would gently break it to Nancy and Ty that we were leaving after breakfast. The hot sun felt wonderful on my face. I dreamed of a new hotel and pictured myself lounging by a beautiful pool, book in hand.

When we arrived at yoga, I quietly stepped onto my mat and let my body flow to Nancy's calm voice. My muscles relaxed with my breath and the tension in my hips had melted away by the time I was in pigeon pose. When savasana came at the end, I almost fell asleep.

I started to have doubts about leaving. The yoga and the food—the chicken curry with vegetables, the flavor-packed grilled fish with fresh mango salsa, the guacamole—were phenomenal. Maybe I could suck it up and deal with the accommodations. After all, we were literally sleeping on the beach.

"Nicole, maybe we should stay?"

She was reclining on her bed, fanning her face with a paperback novel. "Maybe we can stay somewhere up the beach and pop in for the yoga classes," she suggested. I could tell by the grin on her face it was a half-baked plan.

"Telling Nancy and Ty we are staying rather than leaving will be a much easier conversation," I said.

And so we stayed, and I was glad we did.

The next day, some group members and I piled into an old van and took a long, bumpy ride to a cenote, a deep, water-filled sinkhole that is formed when the roof of an underground limestone cavern collapses. It creates a natural pool that is filled by rain and water flowing from underground rivers. We got out of the van, and it looked like we were in the middle of nowhere. The van driver led us through the brush to some steps and we walked gingerly down into a cave. We came upon a 15-foot cliff and took turns jumping into the shimmering aqua waters of the swimming hole, all underground.

Walking to the edge and jumping off the cliff into the beckoning water was exhilarating. I didn't have any moments of panic, I just jumped, knowing all would be OK. I screamed profanities the entire way down while the group cheered me on. I did not think about Jordan or the kids back home. I did not think about Nicole, who had spent the day on the beach. I experienced pure euphoria, enjoying the moment by moment of the day. I was reclaiming my sense of adventure and my sense of self. For a few days, the only person I had to look out for was me.

Afterward, we drove to the Mayan ruins of Coba and climbed the tiny stairs to the top of a pyramid. There, we sat in a circle and each shared something we were grateful for.

"I feel so fortunate to be sitting here on the dusty ground on the top of this ruin in the middle of nowhere with people who were complete strangers to me two days ago," I said with my hands placed in a prayer position at my chest. I marveled at the fact that I was actually there having that experience. It felt unreal.

Nicole stayed back during the outing to relax and connect with her family back home. She spoke to her husband, kids and nanny several times a day. I made one quick call home each day. I loved that we both did what we needed to take care of ourselves. We each did our own thing, yet we still had plenty of time together.

That night I took a salsa dancing class on the beach. We all danced with abandon, soaked to the bone with sweat. After dancing, we moseyed up to the dining hut and engaged in deep discussions about life, religion, afterlife and so much more into the wee hours of the morning. I knew I hungered for real adult conversation, but I realized I needed to make time to fill up my own cup. It was a perfect night. As Nicole and I walked back to our hut, and the moon glistened off the water, I was captivated by beauty I had never imagined when I embarked on this trip.

The rest of the retreat was just as wonderful. I smothered myself from head to toe in bug spray and got used to the insects. We lit our candles each night, took speedy showers, and wore braids and baseball caps during the day. I couldn't wait to crawl into my bug-netted bed at the end of a long, fulfilling day, muscles sore and strong from the yoga. I never got out of my bathing suit or yoga clothes, except on the last night, when I wore a sundress and leggings (to avoid bug bites).

On the last day, we had an ancient Mayan mud ceremony. We placed our arms around one another in a large circle, and I looked deep into the eyes of each person. I could not believe how close I felt to them after our short time together. I was grateful that we hadn't left the retreat or checked into a hotel. I would never have experienced the feelings of joy and living in the moment that I had on the trip. I understood why I was supposed to stay. The bigger picture. I reclaimed my sense of self, the part of me that had been hidden away as I took on the role of mother and wife. I needed to find balance and manage both. I also realized I could adjust my expectations and exceed them in a way I hadn't imagined. I had set out for relaxation, pool time and yoga, and I had gained so much more. I was reawakened. I was reminded of how much I loved adventure and deep discussions and meeting new people through shared experiences. All I'd needed was a reframe and a mindset shift. I renewed the importance of self-care and committed to taking this knowledge home with me. I didn't want to lose this feeling when I set foot on American soil.

And then, we smothered each other in warm and soft mud. We covered our faces, hair, arms and legs. It was slimy and gross and fun all at the same time— something I would not have imagined doing on day one of this trip. We laughed and we ran around on the magical beach like children. Nancy and Ty photographed us as we bonded in the culminating activity of the trip.

Later, this first retreat would seem unreal to me.

The person I was soon to become would appreciate the experience on a different level, yet it was the beginning of a huge shift. I came home transformed. Jordan felt a little left out, but he was happy for me. I chatted easily about my new friends. Nicole and I had developed an even stronger bond.

I was also totally hooked on yoga. I deepened my practice by going to class four or five times per week. I signed up for a yoga intensive training where I was assigned a mentor/teacher, and we worked for an entire weekend in small groups. We broke down the postures and learned about the effects they had on our bodies. We learned advanced postures and practiced inversions like headstands, handstands and crow. I still didn't have an understanding of what yoga was beyond my physical practice. I just knew my body and mind felt amazing when I practiced often.

After our intensives, we would hang out in the studio lobby, drink wine and chat about our lives. I cherished this community and I loved that it was mine. It was my time to figure out who I was and what I wanted. I knew this process began for me in Israel, and though having my babies derailed it a bit, I was focusing on getting to know myself better. I had come a long way from the lost girl in her dorm room who didn't want to leave her parents. I had come a long way from the college graduate who still craved her parents' constant approval. I was following my heart and my own desires. I started to have twinges of desire to become a yoga teacher, or at least go through the year-long training, but it seemed scary to me—could I really do it?

It is better to live your own destiny imperfectly than to imitate someone else's life perfectly.
—THE BHAGAVAD GITA

I sat at my desk watching the snow fall gently outside my large office window. I remembered the days when my kids were little and so excited about a new snowfall. They would jump out of bed, put on their snow pants and winter jackets and race outside to play in the new white blanket. They could spend hours making snowmen or sledding down the hill across the street. Our 55-pound labradoodle, Jazzy, would tear around chasing them as they raced down the hill.

Now, I was alone in the house, all the kids at school. I had a lot of work to do, but I was feeling a little lost, numb. Things were going well with my promotional products business, but I felt like a robot, going through the motions. No thrill, no excitement, no learning, just moving through my day, sending emails, driving carpool, placing work orders, making dinner.

I was discontent almost to the point of feeling sick inside, but I didn't yet know about "my gut" and how connected it was to the way I lived my life. I was finding fault in everyone and everything, but especially in myself: I was not making enough money, I was not successful enough, I was not pretty enough, I was not skinny enough. The list in my hijacked mind went on and on. This was the same list that had gone through my mind when I was young. Perhaps not so surprising since I could still hear my mom's voice, "You should put on a little lipstick," or "How about we get you some highlights?" These messages cut deep and left me feeling inadequate and unattractive.

I loved my mom deeply, but I often felt inferior to her and my family. My parents were glamorous. My brother was drop-dead gorgeous and brilliant. And then there was me: average looks, average smarts, average in personal magnetism and popularity. I couldn't recall my mom ever telling me I was beautiful or smart or strong or brave or any of the adjectives I often used with my own children. Perhaps I hadn't heard her. Maybe my own insecurities and the voices in my head had drowned out any positives I had received.

My current mood wasn't helped by a recent

experience with some of the other moms from my kids' school—women I thought had been my friends. It happened on a girls' trip out west. I'd traveled once before with some of the women in the group, and we had an easy rapport. But this time a new woman, Cassandra, was invited. Cassandra and I weren't close. As soon as she breezed in the door with her rock-sized diamonds and filler-plumped lips, the relaxed vibe of the group vanished. The hair on the back of my neck stood up and my stomach clenched. Was I even breathing? I hadn't yet learned about the wisdom of my gut, so I didn't pay attention to the signs.

Cassandra launched into a monologue about a boy who, it was true, had bullied her son at school on one occasion. "He deserves to be thrown out," she said harshly. "He is trash and so is his family. I think his dad has some sort of shady business."

How could she say that about a 13-year-old who made a dumb adolescent decision? And why was his family trash? Because they were Jewish, and his mom was South American?

"I don't agree with what you're saying," I said, though I would later wonder why. In the moment, it felt right to speak up.

Cassandra fanned herself with her hands. "If it were your son, you'd be upset too," she snapped.

Yes, of course I would, I thought. But I wouldn't trash-talk his family or threaten to withdraw my donations to the school if the child wasn't thrown out, as she had. Absolutely not.

Another woman who I didn't know well spoke up, agreeing with me indirectly by reframing it in the context of her daughter. I wanted to say more, but Cassandra burst into tears, prompting the women to flock to surround her and coo words of comfort. "It's OK, Max will be OK."

The group shot daggered glances my way as I quietly stood, whispered my apologies, and retreated to my bedroom, feeling terrible about making waves and causing a commotion. Somehow this was all my fault.

Back in my room, I took a deep breath, and I called my mom. I wept as I told her what had happened, but she barely heard me—her brother, my uncle Irv, had died. They hadn't been close because he was 20 years older, but she was understandably sad and shaken.

After hanging up with Mom, I thought back to first meeting Cassandra. She moved to the area when her son was in fourth grade and immediately reached out to many of the moms, including me. I was initially impressed by her lavish lifestyle and subtle name dropping. She invited me to go for a walk after our sons' school drop-off one morning and proceeded to talk about herself the entire time. I nodded and said "uh-huh" occasionally, but I may as well have been invisible. During that hour, she did not ask one question about me or take a single pause from talking about herself to get to know me.

It was the same the next time we went for a walk. As she bragged about her money, travels and nonprofit work, I started to feel small. She intimated that I was "financially average," and that I wouldn't understand her plight. Then she changed the subject and said something nice about our sons' friendship.

Our walks left me feeling drained and unimportant. Eventually, Cassandra found a group of friends whose status more closely mirrored hers and got bored with me. It was as if she had brushed me off her shoulder like a pesky bug. And if I had known Cassandra was going to be invited on the girls' trip, I would have declined. Still—and I wish this hadn't been true—I very much wanted to fit in and be a part of this well-connected crowd.

Later that evening, Emily, my roommate, returned to our room.

"What a night!" she said, as if she had enjoyed the drama that unfolded. "She really doesn't like you."

Thank you, I thought. I was well aware.

"You should talk to her tomorrow and clear the air, apologize so it's not awkward for the rest of the trip," Emily said.

Me, apologize?

"OK, I'll try," I said, feeling defeated. I didn't want to make any more waves. I just wanted to get through the next few days without more drama.

"You really upset her, and I don't think she is a woman you want to cross," Emily said.

I couldn't tell if Emily was trying to be kind or if she was enjoying getting mixed up in the drama. We had gotten along well in the past, but now something was telling me not to trust her. I felt like I was in a parallel universe where everyone had gone crazy. Or was I the crazy one? I started to question how I ended up in this ridiculous situation.

The next morning, I awoke in the silky white linens and for a moment forgot where I was. Then it came flooding back to me. I cleaned up and headed out, following the palm tree-lined path to the main house. I took deep breaths as my heart galloped in my chest. I was sure an anxious rash covered my neck as I opened the large door to laughter and chatter. They were all there, and I sensed the mood change as I entered.

"Hey Cassandra, can we chat privately for a minute?" I asked nervously.

"I have no interest in talking with you," she snapped.

"Come on," Emily said. "I'll join you and we'll figure this out."

Pam chimed in, directing her words to me. "You are spoiling this trip for everyone."

I held back tears as Emily, Cassandra and I stepped into one of the expansive bedrooms in the main house.

"I'm so sorry that I offended you last night," I said. "I didn't mean to diminish in any way what happened to Max."

Cassandra looked at me coldly. I felt the sweat pooling in my armpits.

"I'd love for us to be able to put this behind us, move forward and enjoy the day," I said. "I'm probably going to catch a flight home later today." I knew the group would be relieved that I was leaving.

Cassandra puffed herself up. "We will never be friends again."

I felt attacked and tearful. I realized I was OK ending the friendship.

"I am sorry you feel that way," I said. But I wasn't. I wondered what I had been thinking, wanting to become friends with her in the first place. The women in this group were not "my people."

Aside from a few condolences for my uncle, the other women and I didn't interact much before I headed home. I left feeling depleted and shitty. A big social benefit was coming up the next weekend, and I had a feeling I would be the talk of the event. I had a feeling the rumors and stories would get twisted and manipulated and it would all come back to me.

A few days later, I called Nicole. Her son attended a different school, and she didn't know any of the women in the group, except for what I had shared with her over the years.

"What a shit show," she said irritatedly when I told her what had happened. "Why do you hang out with those women?"

The question repeated itself in my head. Why did I hang out with them?

I thought back to my 40th birthday when Nicole and one of my other closest friends, Jessica, organized a surprise birthday dinner with 10 of my close girlfriends. I had no idea the party was happening and was in complete shock when I walked into the cafe and shouts of "SURPRISE!" echoed all around me. There were balloons and some of my favorite faces beaming at me. As we sat around the table, my friends each explained how we first met and shared a funny memory or story from our friendship. I was so touched. It was a perfect birthday. These were the friends I needed to surround myself with. These were the people who lifted me up and truly cared.

So why did I hang out with those other women?

My gut screamed back at me: It's your need to fit in!

When I was in fifth grade, the public school I attended combined kids from fifth and sixth grade into mixed classes. The sixth grade girls in my class mocked me relentlessly—for my pink Guess Jeans with the zippers on the ankles, for my dangly fruit earrings, for being Jewish, for my hair. I didn't have the straight blond hair they all seemed to covet; I had a short curly perm that resembled Little Orphan Annie.

I don't know how the school decided mixing fifth and sixth graders in the same classes was a good idea developmentally. It's a period of developmental explosion for tween-age girls, both in body and mind. It certainly did nothing for me except foster a shrinking sense of self.

My mom spent many mornings in the school office advocating for me, but it accomplished nothing. So she arranged for me to get a makeover from a well-known makeup artist. What I didn't know then was that focusing on what was outside didn't address what was going on inside. While my mom just wanted me to feel better, the message I internalized was that I needed to improve my physical appearance or change who I was to please others.

Change who I was to please others, I thought, as I considered Cassandra and that group of women. This didn't sit well with me. I was an adult, a mother, a small business owner—why would I surround myself with others whose actions made me feel like shit?

I wanted to better understand myself. So I decided to go to therapy.

I felt safe talking to my therapist. She didn't know anything about my past and was interested in what I had to say. She worked in an office with green plants thoughtfully placed around the room—a nice change from my previous therapist's living room. After a few sessions, a light went on, and I realized I needed to start ridding myself of people I did not feel good around. I had to start believing in myself, to better recognize and value my own gifts and talents. I knew this would be much easier said than done. But I was committed to starting that journey, wherever it would take me.

My therapist suggested I call Pam, the organizer of the girls' trip and whose company in the past I had thoroughly enjoyed. She hadn't spoken to me since the trip she said I had spoiled for everyone. I had sent her a handwritten thank you/apology note when I returned, but she hadn't said more than a quick "hello" as she breezed past me at school drop-offs. My therapist thought a phone call would either open the door for communication and repair or provide some sort of closure to the relationship.

I didn't like confrontation in general, particularly with people I knew were upset with me. Nonetheless, I called her cell.

"Hi Pam, it's Marnie. Can we talk?" My heart pounded in my ears.

"What's up?" she said, her voice flat.

"I'd like to talk about what happened on the trip. I want to tell you how sorry I am that things went down the way they ..."

"You know what, Marnie?" she interrupted. "I don't have time or space in my life for people like you and your drama."

I was so taken aback I wasn't sure what to say. I felt tears coming. Maybe there was something wrong with me. These women wanted nothing to do with me. I gazed out the window at the beautiful succulents on my back patio and thought about how simple their existence was.

"OK," I said quietly.

There was nothing left to say. I hung up the phone dumbfounded. She was not even willing to listen. It was clear how little she cared about me or our supposed friendship.

My therapist assured me that closure was a good thing. She instructed me write in a notebook 10 times in a row: "People like me for who I am" and "What I have to say is important." I did this exercise for a long time, and somewhere deep inside me, I started to sense the shift in my mindset. I filled pages and pages with those mantras until I believed the words. And finally, I was ready to close the door on those thoughtless women.

**A journey of a thousand miles
begins with a single step.
—LAO TZU**

Therapy taught me a great deal about who I was and who I wanted to be, but I still felt down. My gut had twisted into a permanent knot, and my neck and shoulders were always tense. I sat in my office staring out the window. I lit a candle, and in its calming flicker I tried to discern what was really going on inside me. What I knew in my bones was that my promotions company was not making me happy anymore. When I first started, closing a sale was so fulfilling. Contributing financially to our family provided a great sense of self-worth. But slowly, the excitement melted away. Clients could be rude and demanding. They didn't understand the printing process despite my efforts to educate them. Some clients were taking advantage of me. My one-stop-shop was on the smaller side, so I never wanted to turn orders away. Which meant I often ended up working on less-than-desirable projects with difficult people.

"I need more!" my body screamed at me.

But what was that more?

I had always been interested in health and wellness. I scoured magazines and newspaper articles and followed lots of alternative medicine doctors on the Internet. I was a book junkie and read every health and wellness book that interested me. Maybe I could get a master's degree in health and wellness? Was that even a thing?

I had made it through part of the master's in business communications at the University of St. Thomas before following Jordan to Israel. Now I wondered why I'd given up on my dreams. I wasn't sure how much I cared about my career and my passions when I was in my early 20s. A part of me just wanted to get married and have babies. Or it may have been what I thought was expected of me. No one ever came out and said it, but it was what my mom did, and her mom, and her mom. Like the women in my family for generations, I would be a stay-at-home mom who put all her time and energy into her kids.

I was no longer that younger version of myself, willing to set everything aside for Jordan or to fulfill others' expectations. I still wanted to spend a lot of quality time with my kids, who brought me so much pleasure and joy, but I yearned for more. What did I want to do?

It was 2014, five years after the transformative beach yoga retreat in Tulum. I started researching my interests: health, wellness, yoga, business, holistic, alternative. I searched every word that resonated with me. As I searched, "coach" popped up repeatedly—it was as if the word had found me. I had done a lot of listening, coaching and advising in my personal life. I coached friends on issues with their spouses or children. I listened to my mom vent about her troubles. I advised my own kids on various problems regarding friendships or school. Listening intently was one of my strengths.

As I continued to search, I came across a field called health coaching, a term I had never heard before. It was exactly what I was looking for. And just like that, I decided to go back to school. The thought alone made me giddy with excitement. I wanted to scream from the rooftop, "I have a purpose! I am doing something interesting!" I couldn't wait to tell Jordan and the kids.

"I'm going back to school to be a health coach!" I piped up excitedly at dinner.

"What does that mean?" Zach asked.

"I'm going to help people live happier and healthier lives," I said, smiling broadly.

"Cool," Zach said.

Jordan smiled. "I think Mom will really enjoy this!"

And then dinner went on as usual, none of us really having a clue what my becoming a health coach would mean or look like. But I didn't feel nervous about what it meant. My gut was telling me I could do it and everything would work out. I felt the best I had in a long time. It was as if I were floating. That week, I registered for a 15-month course at the Institute for Integrative Nutrition (IIN).

Two months into my coursework, my friend Julie and I met to paddleboard on Lake Minnetonka, one of my favorite lakes in the Twin Cities area. As we paddled through the calm water on a beautiful summer afternoon, I told her about my quest for self-discovery and the health coaching course.

"I'm hoping to figure out who I am and how I can do what I'm meant to do in this world," I said.

She was on a similar journey to find her purpose, and we bounced ideas off one another. We discussed women-led businesses, health coaching, college counseling, writing books. I pictured owning a coaching business and helping clients on their journeys to better health. I imagined giving lectures to a full house and becoming a published author. My mind was flooded with possibilities. As I paddled, I breathed in the fresh summer air and felt an immense sense of gratitude and contentment.

Then Julie mentioned YogaCalm®, a yoga program geared toward school-aged children for social, emotional and therapeutic purposes. It immediately piqued my interest. I had always been comfortable around kids and teenagers. Perhaps because I'd spent many Saturday nights babysitting as a teen. I had also been a camp counselor, and enjoyed leading the campers, singing silly songs, making up games, sitting in the grass eating lunch. When I was around kids, I felt like I could be myself, that I was more than enough for them. I never worried about what the kids thought of me and that felt good. Even as an adult, I loved (and still do) spending time with teenagers and young adults. Being around them made me feel like a kid at heart. I enjoyed the energy, enthusiasm and sense of adventure young people possessed.

As soon as I got home from paddleboarding, I researched YogaCalm® and discovered there was a teacher training program starting the following month. It was three full weekend workshops, followed by a practicum where participants learned from and taught under another certified teacher for 20 hours. For the final project, I would have to submit a written class plan that I had created. This all seemed doable. The last part about submitting a recording of myself teaching my class to students terrified me. I'd never liked how I looked or sounded on camera. How would I remember the words? What if I wasn't good enough? All my insecurities rushed back.

But my good old gut, which was becoming my friend, nagged back. I was noticing the feelings deep within me and realized I felt better when I listened to and acted on my internal voice and desires. I'd thought about participating in a yoga teacher training for a long time. My gut told me this could be a safe first step.

I enrolled immediately, before I lost the nerve. Everyone thought I was crazy participating in two programs at once, health coaching certification and YogaCalm®, while simultaneously running ChillyBean Promotions and caring for my three kids. But the two programs complemented each other, and I was already a student, so adding another course seemed logical. Plus, life was getting easier. Gabi, my youngest, was now 8 years old. I had more time to pursue my interests. I would pursue my education now, so I could launch my new career as my kids got older. I was setting the stage.

What I didn't know at the time was that my thirst for knowledge wouldn't stop there. I never wanted my education to end. I loved to learn and found many topics interesting. I enjoyed learning about people, their cultures, their pasts and their stories. I imagine myself as a retired person, taking classes alongside people in their 20s, keeping my mind and spirit sharp.

For the first weekend of YogaCalm® teacher training, I drove across the Mississippi River from Minneapolis to its sister city, St. Paul. The only time I ventured to St. Paul was for a concert or to go to the theater. As I entered the studio, I didn't know a soul. I immediately felt out my comfort zone, which usually meant I would lose my words—my chest would tighten, my neck would break out in a rash, and my mind would go blank. I grabbed a coursebook, a mat, and the gear the instructor had laid out for us and found a space in the front row. I sat quietly on my mat and listened to the chatter surrounding me. Others seemed to know one another. Why was I always the person in a room who didn't know a soul? As I second-guessed my decision to be there, my thoughts were interrupted by the instructor, Rosie, who started with a welcome meditation. My muscles released with ease.

Introductions came next. As the reality of giving my elevator pitch set in, I felt sweat soak my armpits. Despite being in a room filled with educators, yogis and therapists—some of the most disarming people on the planet—my heart started pounding. My cheeks burned with embarrassment and the rash bloomed on my neck like an ugly ink blot. It was a reaction I expected and detested. Why did my skin have to spill my secrets?

As others introduced themselves, I took deep breaths to calm myself. It didn't work. When it was my turn, I gave my spiel quickly, leaving out important details. I didn't share why I was taking the class like others had. I didn't share what my passions or goals were. I didn't even mention my business. I shared that I had three kids, as if motherhood was the only thing that defined me, or the only part of me worthy of mention. I was relieved when the next person spoke and the attention was focused on someone else.

As I began to obsess about how I needed to find my voice, Rosie's voice interrupted my thoughts. "Stand up with your legs spread apart," she said.

I followed her lead, standing with my knees

slightly bent, and then clasped my hands together, and raised them over my head.

"We'll work on the movement first and then add the sound," Rosie said.

She counted to three and, bright-eyed, exclaimed, "Hands clasped, swing down through your legs like you are chopping wood, and then lift your arms back above your head—do this three times."

As I swung my arms wildly up and down, I thought about the kids I would teach this move to eventually. I thought of leading the campers through silly exercises back when I was a camp counselor. Little did I know I would one day demonstrate this exact move to underprivileged kids in schools and inpatient teens on the psych ward at the University of Minnesota Hospital.

"The sound is a deep, guttural HUH!" Rosie said. "It comes from the depths of your core and soul. As you swing down, the sound matches your movement."

I glanced around the room and thought, are we really doing this? Rosie was the kind of person I wanted to emulate. She had captured the group's attention first with the welcome meditation and now with this exercise that was clearly meant to release our anxieties. I mimicked her moves, giving it my all as I yelled "HUH!" I became so focused on the present, the movement and the sound, that I completely forgot about being self-conscious. My body felt relaxed and free, like a caged animal that had just been released.

I began to feel more confident. I connected with a woman named Emma, who was also a mom making the trek from the western suburbs into St. Paul. During our short lunch breaks, Emma and I would chat about our lives. I learned she had already completed her 200-hour yoga certification and was teaching classes at a small local studio. I instantly admired her. She came to class in her Birkenstock sandals, no make-up, a colorful woven messenger bag slung over her shoulder. She spoke with authority and was clearly comfortable in her own skin.

The weekend trainings were spread out over a few months. In between those weekends, there was coursework and physical work to complete that would count toward my teaching practicum. This was the space where I excelled—doing the work in my own space and on my own time.

I set up a studio in the basement and began leading a YogaCalm® class for my youngest and most forgiving child, Gabi. The ceilings were low in the basement, but the walls were painted a cheery yellow to keep it bright and light, and one wall was mirrored. I had learned the importance of having a focal object for the kids to look at, so I used a colorful Hoberman sphere, otherwise known as the breathing ball. I would light a candle, dim the lights, and tap a chime gently to get the practice session started.

Gabi listened intently, and I felt like I was giving her a gift by teaching her to breathe and to regulate her emotions through movement at such a young age. She seemed to enjoy our sessions together and would hang on my every word as she followed my lead. She was excited when I suggested we invite a few of her friends to join in on the practice.

I noticed immediately how Gabi took the breathing techniques into her own life. She had a terrible fear of shots and needles (like her mama) and when it was time for her flu shot, she closed her eyes and took big, deep, calming belly breaths. I couldn't help but smile, thankful for the tools I had been able to share with her.

As I continued working through the YogaCalm® teacher training coursework and the health coach training, I noticed a bounce in my step. I felt a "joie de vivre" I had not felt in a long time. I thought of my time living in Israel when I slowly came into my own. I began to understand this was what life was—a series of awakenings, small steps that eventually led us to our most true selves.

The IIN coursework dove deeply into nutritional theories. I learned about bio-individuality and primary and secondary foods. I learned about the 90/10 rule developed by health and nutrition expert Joy Bauer. To balance food intake, the rule called for eating 90 percent healthy, nutritious food, and indulging in less healthy food 10 percent of the time. I studied digestion and the disorders that go along with digestive issues. I developed a deeper understanding of how the body and the mind work together. I learned the best ways to engage others about health, so they'd feel comfortable sharing their concerns. I was introduced to complementary alternative medical modalities such as Ayurveda from the Indian traditions, acupuncture, aromatherapy, reiki and more.

I was thrilled that what I was learning in both my nutrition and yoga training was complementary—it all overlapped and fit together. It made me wish I had paid more attention during ninth grade biology class, when I skipped the pig dissection because I was a vegetarian, and then proceeded to fail the test. I realized I would have appreciated and enjoyed learning that so much more now, as I was coming to understand how the body works, and how what we do with and put into our bodies affects our health and wellness.

What I was learning also inspired me to make changes at home. I started with myself and gave up gluten first, to see if I would notice a difference. Earlier that year, I developed a nasty rash on my stomach a dermatologist diagnosed as Grover's disease, an allergic-type skin condition that typically affects middle-aged men. There were no good treatment options, so I took matters into my own hands and began doing research. I read dozens of articles and learned the skin is highly permeable and can manifest symptoms of inflammation and toxicity at the surface of the body. I searched for alternative modalities to treat it, something I would not have done a year earlier. I discovered giving up gluten could be helpful, so I gave it a whirl. I also read that heat treatments, like a hot shower followed by blowing hot air on it from a hair dryer, could help. Within eight weeks of these combined treatments, my rash was completely gone. I would eventually do food sensitivity testing on myself, and the results would register a low level of sensitivity to gluten. I learned I could eat high-quality gluten and wheat-containing products in small doses, but when I ate too much of it, I would break out in a rash on my trunk. And when I cut back on the gluten again, it quickly resolved.

In addition to eliminating gluten myself, I cut down on the crackers, chips, sweets and processed foods in our cabinets at home, swapping them out for healthier alternatives. I focused on cooking with a rainbow of foods that came from the earth. I experimented with many ways of healing my body from the inside out. Gone were the days of turning to an external beauty regime to fix what didn't feel right inside.

What I really appreciated about IIN were the like-minded people I met in the program from all over the world. I had classmates from Mexico, India, Israel, England, Australia. I was thrilled to be pulled out of my small world and into their experiences. Each student was paired with an accountability partner and placed into mastermind groups, which I had never heard of before the course. Masterminds offered a combination of education, brainstorming, peer accountability and support in a group setting, and were intended to sharpen both business and personal skills. Members challenged each other to set strong goals, and more importantly, to accomplish them.

My accountability partner, Beth, was from New

York City. She was a food journalist for Women's Health magazine and a recipe developer and had already written and published a few cookbooks. Initially, I felt inadequate being partnered with her, but after our first phone call, any insecurities I had had vanished. Beth was lovely and caring. She had her own stresses and experienced emotions that were similar to the ones I had. The fact that I was from Minneapolis and had no experience in health coaching didn't seem to faze her. Beth and I formed a strong bond, coaching and advising one another on personal issues and giving each other suggestions regarding business. I found comfort in knowing I was not alone on my journey to self-discovery.

Toward the end of 15 months, IIN was hosting a weekend conference—it was the culmination of the program. Students would come together from all around the world for a live event in New York at the Jazz at Lincoln Center concert venue. The speaker list included IIN founder Joshua Rosenthal, Vani Hari (aka The Food Babe), Geneen Roth, Dr. David Katz and Paul Pitchford.

The conference was scheduled for April, the same month as my birthday, so Jordan and I decided to head to Manhattan together a few days before the event and called it my birthday trip. I planned for an entire six days away. We would see a musical on Broadway, visit the 911 memorial and museum, shop and explore the city. Then Jordan would fly home when the conference began.

I hadn't been there in the spring. I felt so alive as we walked the streets, with the tulips in bloom throughout the city. Our time together was wonderful, and after Jordan left, I was thankful to have a few days to myself; I had become so much more independent than I was during our college days and early in our time living in Israel. I looked forward to finding all the healthy little cafés, juice bars and hip boutique yoga studios. I didn't worry about eating alone or roaming the streets by myself, I reveled in the solitude. I hadn't realized how much I needed the trip. I was grateful for time to focus solely on caring for myself and a reprieve from the exhaustion of motherhood and being the manager of the family schedule. I had been longing for days without the colored blocks of activities filling up my Google calendar—carpools, practices, rehearsals. I was beginning to realize that self-care was not selfish. I noticed that when I met my own needs, and felt happy and content, I was a better person all around.

The conference space was majestic and invigorating and gave me the chills. I had never been surrounded by so many like-minded people. I was accustomed to being the "health nut" among my family and friends—an outlier. I was the one who said "no thank you" to many sweets and meats and heavily processed foods. But at the conference, I felt like I fit right in.

I made small talk with the women sitting near me throughout the morning sessions. After lunch, I reached out to members of my mastermind group to see if they wanted to meet up. They added me to a group chat and invited me to join them for dinner at a vegan restaurant that evening. I met a woman named Rachel from Canada with a nose ring and naturally beautiful inner glow and invited her to join the group for dinner. She was an astronomer by day and hoped to transition to full-time holistic health coach. She didn't have a spouse or children and was spending her spare time working on launching her business. She had already been a guest on a few podcasts and radio shows, chatting about health and wellness. I was so impressed. Podcasts were barely on my radar at that time, and I certainly hadn't thought about talking on a podcast.

I appreciated so many moments on the trip. At one point I thought, "Look at you now! Just a few months ago, you were despondent. Now here you are in New York City, attending a conference on your own, hanging out with and learning from and being inspired by people you just met!" If someone had told me a year earlier that was what I would be doing, I would have told them they were crazy.

When my son, Zach, and my niece were little, my dad created what he called the Rulebreaker Club. It began when he and my mom would let the kids stay up past their bedtimes, eat popcorn, and break other minor rules. There was even a secret handshake, and I had Rulebreaker Club T-shirts made for everyone. It was about more than breaking the rules. It was about living outside of the confines of societal norms to be who you truly are. Even a healthy deviant is a rule breaker. The IIN conference showed me that I was learning to dismantle the rigid guidelines I had set for myself throughout my life and was becoming my own kind of rule breaker.

**Breathe in deeply to bring your mind
home to your body.
—THICH NHAT HANH**

"Why do you do this to yourself?" my mom asked as I described my busy schedule and coursework.

I was in the midst of earning my health coaching and YogaCalm® certifications when I enrolled in one more program—230-hour yoga teacher training. It made perfect sense to me. The programs were interconnected. They were all helping me figure out what I believed, what I wanted, who I was. They were helping me answer deep questions in different ways. It was as if a magnetic force was guiding me. My gut was talking to me again, and I was listening.

As my journey of learning continued, my home life improved tremendously. I found myself more patient with my kids, more interested in being present with them. I was more understanding of Jordan and his needs and desires, aware of how we differed, that we sometimes wanted and needed different things. I noticed when I filled my cup with my own interests, I wasn't as bothered by his workaholic tendencies.

The first time I went to visit Jordan in Los Angeles was just after our freshman year of college. He wanted me to meet his family and show me around LA. We took a boat ride to Catalina Island, and he puked over the side the entire way back. But that wasn't the worst of it. For me, the worst part of the trip was when he talked about applying to med school and wanting to be a doctor since he was 15, and when he said, "Marnie you're not a very motivated or driven person."

This sent me into a serious tizzy. I considered myself highly motivated and resourceful, and in that one statement I thought, "This guy clearly does not know me!"

We got into a huge fight. After I flew home, I broke up with him. We were separated for four months. Then, once we were back at school, I was finally ready to give him another chance. I'm happy I did, but I am also glad I stood up for myself.

Jordan certainly didn't see me as someone who lacked motivation anymore.

The timing of my decision to start the 230-hour yoga teacher training was also influenced by the instructor and the location. A woman I looked up to tremendously, Betsy, was going to be the lead teacher in the program. The class was in downtown Minneapolis, in the North Loop, and I yearned for an experience outside of the suburbs where I spent most of my time.

I called Betsy before signing up. I asked basic questions about the program and logistics. I explained that I was not planning to teach in a studio, that for me, the training was self-discovery and gaining knowledge. She said that while many students entered the training for similar reasons, I might change my mind as I enveloped myself deeper into the 15-month program.

The training was a much larger commitment to yoga than I'd made up to that point. It was four and a half hours of training every week—three with Betsy, and one and a half with the other teachers—plus three full weekend workshops. Additionally, once my training was complete, I would have to participate in a mentorship program, and then find a community teaching setting where I would volunteer teach and put into practice everything I learned.

I quickly decided I was in. I also knew exactly where I wanted to volunteer teach—Jewish Family and Children's Service of Minneapolis, an organization that provides services to people in need of all ages, religions and backgrounds. The thought of teaching on my own made me nervous, but I had a few months to prepare, so I aimed to learn as much as I could before then.

Wednesday nights were my favorite of the week. I would make a quick dinner for the family while the kids sat at the counter and chatted and worked on homework. Then at 5:30 p.m., I would tell them with excitement, "It's time for me to head out to my training class!"

I looked forward to the drive into Minneapolis, the way the city rose up ahead in the distance as I zipped along on the freeway. When the weather was nice, I would blast the stereo and roll down the windows, and the wind would whip my hair around. My shoulders would relax into the driver's seat as my body transitioned from mom and business owner to yoga teacher trainee.

The North Loop neighborhood was always vibrant, with its hip boutiques and restaurants, and live music outdoors along the Mississippi Riverfront. The sidewalks were full of couples walking hand-in-hand, joggers whizzing by with their dogs, and businesspeople dashing from old warehouse buildings that had been converted into office space. I'd park on the street a few blocks from the studio, in front of red brick townhouses with tiny terraces. As I walked to the training, I would pass the residents sitting on their patios, talking and laughing, and soak in the energy of a world completely different from my own.

By the time I arrived at the studio, I was invigorated and relaxed all at once. I'd ring the buzzer to enter the building and step into the elevator—the clunky old-fashioned kind you wouldn't want to get stuck in—and ride it slowly up to the second floor. The studio would embrace me with the scent of essential oils like lavender, mint or lemon. A small boutique in the front of the building sold yoga mats, blocks and straps, an extensive collection of books, soy candles and hand-crafted jewelry.

I bought my first Mala bead necklace from the boutique—a string of 108 green, blue, pink and multi-colored beads anchored by a slightly larger burnt orange bead, each stone tied with a red knot between it. The significance of 108 beads is left to interpretation. Some say there are 108 energy lines connected to the heart—one of them is believed to be the path to self-realization. I did not yet know how Mala beads were used for mantra and meditation. I was immediately drawn to the fact that the necklace was handmade by a local artisan. And for me, it represented protection—for my family and me. I had never been a superstitious person, but I began taking the necklace with me whenever I traveled. Even now, anytime I get on an airplane, I bring my Mala beads. I rarely wear them as a necklace; instead I wrap them tightly around my wrist.

The first day of yoga teacher training, I was awed by the beauty of the second floor studio. It reminded me of the dance studio in the '80s movie "Flashdance." Its large floor-to-ceiling windows were streaked with late-day sun, and the old, warped hardwood floors creaked beneath my feet. As I looked around, I realized I was once again in a room with no one I knew. It had become a pattern, and I was beginning to wonder if perhaps I enjoyed challenging myself that way—putting myself out there, outside of my comfort zone. There were only five other people in the class, which was more my speed. The instructor, Betsy, had not yet arrived, so we briefly introduced ourselves and sat quietly waiting for class to start.

At the last minute, Betsy arrived. She had the friendliest face, wild, curly brown hair and soft brown eyes. I didn't know her well, but we had some mutual friends, and back in high school, she hung out with my brother. After formal introductions, she jumped right in and talked about mantra—or "muntra," as she pronounced it. I knew the word but didn't know its deeper meaning. Betsy taught us it can be incredibly powerful. It is a word or words chanted or sung as an incantation or prayer. It can also be self-affirming statements for strength and confidence to face the world. But its underlying purpose is to help focus the attention and calm the mind of the person chanting it. As I listened to Betsy's explanation, the notion of a mind calmed and empowered through song made me feel peaceful.

Betsy proceeded to gift our class with a mantra called "Mahamrityunjaya Mantra," which is considered the most powerful shiva mantra, for longevity and warding off untimely death. It also removes fears and heals holistically. On that first day, she sang it for us. As the lead singer in a '70s and '80s cover band called Stereo Kitchen, Betsy was used to getting up on the stage and belting out songs and dancing. It was something I had known about her before taking the class and one of the things I admired about her. It was one of the reasons I was excited to have her as my yoga mentor—I hoped some of her fearlessness would rub off on me.

We sat in a line, cross-legged on our yoga mats, facing the gorgeous windows, eyes closed and forearms resting on our knees, our fingers positioned into a common hand mudra. Mudra, a Sanskrit word, is a symbolic hand gesture with the power to produce joy and happiness. In this case, the gesture symbolized knowledge; thumb and pointer finger connected to make a circle, remaining fingers extended outward.

"Aum Tryambakam yajaamahe sugandhim pushtivardhanam," Betsy sang. "Urvaarukamiva bandhanaan-mrityormuksheeya maamritaat."

Its meaning: "We worship the three-eyed one who is fragrant, and who sustains all living beings. May he liberate us from (Samsara) death. May he (Lord Shiva) lead us to immortality, just as the cucumber is released from its bondage."

Chills tingled down my spine as I listened to the beautiful song and took in its meaning. In that moment, I knew I was right where I was supposed to be.

To learn the Sanskrit words, we chanted them repeatedly. When it was time to sing the words, all my fears emerged. I was a sixth grader in music class all over again, being told something was wrong with my singing voice. Thoughts of the doctor telling my mom I would never be a professional singer bubbled to the surface—I could almost hear his condescending laugh.

I loved to sing when I was alone or with my kids. I

had no problem belting out show tunes in the shower, or as I raced across the lake on a jet ski, or in the car on the way to school with my girls. I wanted my kids to know there was no shame in using their voices and singing loudly and proudly. I signed my daughters up for voice lessons and told their teacher I had a terrible voice but loved to sing. I asked if she would work with me as well. I learned that because I had not been exposed to music at a young age, I would have to work harder. I would sing along with my daughter, Gabi, and found I could match her pitch better than I could a piano. I felt most comfortable singing with her and she also gave me lots of encouragement.

"Mom, your voice is pretty!" she said. "And you can hit such high notes!"

Her words meant a lot to me and gave me the extra boost of confidence to keep going.

I worked on the Italian song "Caro Mio Ben" with the teacher, and found not only could I sing it, but I was also proud of how I sounded when I did.

"Fabulous job, Marnie!" the teacher exclaimed. "Will you sing it at our end of year recital?"

"No way!" I said, not confident enough yet to sing publicly.

My combined trainings had helped me find and develop my voice. My voice was strong. But many times, my nerves got the better of me. With my anxiety came a nagging, negative voice that would try to override my strong voice and insist that what it had to stay wasn't important.

That nagging, negative voice had been there a long time. It started in my early teens, when I would race through the back door after school, excited to share all the details of my day with my mom—from the conversations I had and which classes were boring, to what I ate for lunch and what other kids were wearing.

"Honey, can you please stop talking," she said. "I can't even hear myself think."

Later, at the dinner table, I would try again.

"Marnie, sha!" my dad would say as he discussed business with my mom.

When my eyeliner-wearing brother with his spiked hair spoke, my parents sat up and gave him their full attention, practically hanging on his every word.

"Why are you so excited to hear what Louie has to say, but not what I have to say?" I asked.

"You talk a mile a minute and Louie rarely speaks," my mom said. "What he has to say is usually worth listening to."

This crushed me. When I asked her about it

many years later as an adult, her response was just as hurtful: "You talked a lot and I honestly found it annoying at times."

So at a young age, I started sharing less and holding back. And over the years, my silenced voice had become like a dormant volcano.

During yoga teacher training, I noticed early on that my silenced voice began to come to life. When it was my turn to lead my classmates through a sun salutation, initially I worried I would say the wrong words with the wrong postures. But I had been practicing for years and could do the sun salutations in my sleep. I worried my classmates might see the sweat dripping from my armpits, or notice my hands shaking, or hear my voice wavering. Now I was in a safe space, surrounded by people who valued what I had to say. As I led my classmates through the simple salutations, the negative, nagging voice was silenced. And then came the feedback.

"Nice job."

"Your voice was soothing."

"I liked your pace."

I felt empowered. I felt like I was bursting into my future, finally becoming who I was meant to be.

My teaching confidence continued to grow. When I taught my first community class for Jewish

Family and Children's Service, four students came, and only one of them had practiced very basic yoga. I asked if anyone had injuries and they told me about their various aches and pains—this one had tight hamstrings, that one had a sore shoulder. I had planned a restorative class, which would be great for the group, but I hadn't considered how challenging it would be to cue them into postures as they heard the Sanskrit words and posture names for the first time.

I took a deep breath and shut out the negative voice.

"Stand with your feet shoulder-width apart and ground or plant your feet into the earth," I instructed. "Make sure all four corners of your feet are pressed into the mat and wiggle your toes."

The group followed my lead.

"Now bring your hands to your heart and close your eyes," I continued rhythmically. "And let's start by taking some deep breaths in—one, two, three, four, and out—one, two, three, four."

As I instructed my students to breathe, I inhaled and exhaled along with them, and I started to feel the true power of my own breath.

**I am not the same, having seen the moon
shine on the other side of the world.
—MARY ANNE RADMACHER**

After more than 36 hours of travel and changing planes in multiple cities, we finally landed in Zimbabwe. We retrieved our luggage at the tiny airport and headed to the hotel perched on the edge of the Zambezi River and gorge. It was the beginning of our family trip of a lifetime in honor of my parents' 50th wedding anniversary.

The next day, as I took in the views surrounding the hotel, I saw the mist of the famous Victoria Falls in the distance and the giant bridge separating Zimbabwe from neighboring Zambia. Small warthogs wandered the property, casually grazing in the grass. Large dung beetles rolled balls of animal poop the size of softballs across the lawn.

As we ventured out to see Victoria Falls up close, we followed the trail through all the lookout points. It was indescribably beautiful. The jungle was thick with trees and foliage, and the waterfalls were stunning. The spray coming off the falls was constant and heavy like a rainstorm under completely blue skies. It felt good in the muggy heat.

We took our time wandering down the trail, soaked to the bone. Rainbows were everywhere we looked and at each turn on the trail. It may have been the first time I had ever seen my parents take their time. I took photo after photo, unable to truly capture the magnitude and beauty of this natural wonder of the world. I wished I could bottle it and save it forever, the sheer beauty surrounding me.

My awe was mixed with fear. Along the trail, there were steep cliffs without railings, and I imagined my three children and my niece taking a wrong, slippery step and falling to their deaths. My motherly instinct kicked in several times as I warned the kids to stay away from the edge. With his fear of heights, I didn't worry about Jordan getting too close to the edge.

Despite being anxious about the edges, I never wanted to leave, to let go of this otherworldly feeling. My life back in Minneapolis seemed like a distant memory, a tiny speck in a faraway place I used to know.

As we made our way back to the hotel on the narrow dirt trail, we were surrounded by local artisans selling their wares. We purchased hand-carved figurines to take home to remind us of our travels.

After lunch, we headed out for our next adventure, zip-lining across the giant gorge along the Zambezi, the fourth largest river in Africa, which was filled with crocodiles. From where we stood in Zimbabwe, we gazed across the river to Zambia. My niece went first, and as I watched her, my knees shook. I knew if I did not go next, I would not go at all. Standing on the ledge ready to step off the platform, I was filled with terror. I pushed through my fear and jumped, screaming the whole way down. As my zip line slowed, I composed myself and took in the surroundings. I was gliding though the air in the middle of a gorge with beautiful birds and spectacular views all around me. The Zambezi rushed below. I took in a deep breath, savoring the moment; I knew it would not last, and it would never happen again.

After everyone else had taken a turn, Gabi decided not to go. Though she was only 8, she knew her limits and stuck to her guns. Eleven-year-old Sage took a second turn in her sister's place. She went in tandem with Jordan who, despite his incredible fear of heights, made the leap with his daughter by his side.

While I'd had my fill of adventure for the day, my son, my niece and my brother had not. They had planned to do a 365-foot bungee jump off the enormous Victoria Falls bridge, which was built in 1904 over the second gorge of Victoria Falls. Everything about it made me nervous. My gut screamed not to let them go, but I silenced my inner voice and did not try to talk them out of it.

To get to the bungee site, we crossed border control and walked a half-mile to the bridge, midway between official Zimbabwe and Zambia territory. It was a long, slow and incredibly hot walk. We were surrounded by Zimbabwean women who glided by with colorful baskets on their heads, and men zipping around on rickety old bikes. Each time a truck passed, the entire bridge shook and bounced. My anxiety continued to build as we made our way across.

When we arrived at the site, those who planned to bungee jump were required to sign a waiver. My sense of reason melted in the humidity. What if something happened? Was I putting my family in danger? What if I never got to hug my son, Zach, again? My heart felt like it might burst out of my body.

I held my breath as my niece jumped and then

Zach. Once back on firm ground, the kids bubbled with enthusiasm about their experience and how much they had loved it. I made Zach promise he wouldn't bungee jump again—at least not in my presence, and not until after he'd turned 18.

The next morning, before boarding a small plane to South Africa, we packed up and walked toward Victoria Falls one final time to shop at the marketplace. As we headed out, a mama warthog and four piglets blocked our path. I marveled at an up-close view of them in their natural habitat. I could have watched for hours, but it was time to move on. We purchased trinkets for the kids at the market, and as we began to walk back, a large guard stopped us at the foot of the trail. He informed us that a wild Cape buffalo with a calf was a few yards away. Our eyes followed his finger to an enormous buffalo peering back at us.

"It could charge at any time," the guard said. "It is not safe to walk this way."

My thoughts raced. All the materials from the travel agent had advised against wearing brightly colored clothing because it attracted animals. Today had been deemed a travel day, so we hadn't thought about it, and Zach was wearing a fluorescent yellow shirt. The guard motioned rapidly for Zach to take off his shirt as the buffalo stared him down. The guard motioned for us to follow as he led us off the path. The thick brush scratched our arms as we made our way through the deep jungle quietly, carefully. Each step was more cautious than the next. I wondered if I was taking my last steps. Once the buffalo was out of sight, we paused briefly. I started to catch my breath. I had no idea how far we'd just walked.

As the guard led us back to a narrow trail, a troop of about two dozen baboons walked toward us on the trail in a single file line. They ranged in size from large males to little babies grasping their mother's hands. Was I imagining this? Like classmates passing in the school hallway. They were so close I could have reached out to touch them. I could not believe my eyes. It was truly magnificent and terrifying at the same time. And it happened so fast; I didn't have time to process what I had just witnessed.

When at last we made it to the hotel gate, relief swept over me like a tidal wave. We frantically grabbed our bags and made it just in time to the airport, ready for our next adventure.

From the moment the tiny airplane landed on the minuscule strip of runway at the Mala Mala Game Reserve in South Africa, my anticipation built as I imagined what the next five days would bring. The reserve was located on the edge of Kruger National Park, sandwiched between the park and the Sabi Sand Game Reserve.

Park rangers Nicolaas and Marius greeted us as we stepped off the plane. We had lunch and got settled in our huts, and then piled into two open safari Jeeps to tour the African bush. We learned this particular reserve was home to the "big five"—lions, leopards, rhinoceroses, elephants and Cape buffalo. I tried to contain my worry as I explained to the kids we would be very close to wild animals, and it was important to follow whatever rules Nicolaas and Marius laid out for us. In response, they bubbled with excitement—I hoped what I said had actually sunk in.

Not two minutes after leaving camp, our Jeep came to a stop.

"There is a female leopard asleep in the tree," Marius whispered, pointing to a giant sleeping cat above us and just 10 feet away. "Stay calm and don't make any sudden movements."

My face sunk into a frown and I slunk low in my seat. The kids were in awe of the leopard and quietly asked Marius questions.

"Why is she in the tree?"

"Will she come down?"

"What does she think of the safari Jeep?"

I glanced over at the second Jeep, where the rest of my family looked relaxed and seemed to find my fear amusing. Their mocking subsided when a male leopard jumped down from another a tree and landed right next to our Jeep. He was so close I could have touched him. As he circled the vehicle, I prayed that Sage and Gabi, who were seated in the back row all by themselves, would not become his lunch. The leopard moseyed past the Jeeps as if he didn't have a care in the world.

After a period of quiet observation, we moved on. We went on to see Cape buffalo, elephants, impalas, hippos, lions and a black rhino. We learned so much about the animals witnessing them in nature. It made me keenly aware of the delicateness of life, and how some animals were meant to eat others in order to maintain nature's balance.

Our guide Marius was born and raised in South Africa. He was a naturalist and a survivalist, and described how he was drawn to the bush. He answered our questions about his life, his education and his job. I had never met anyone with so much excitement for and devotion to the land and the animals; he made it easy to get swept up in the moment. It made me reflect on my own path and how I felt about my work and my day-to-day life; it ignited a fire in me to continue pursuing my passions.

We stayed in the bush until the sun dropped below the horizon, rich oranges, yellows and reds illuminating the sky around us. As it turned pitch black, we listened to nighttime sounds like African singing frogs, "Bubbling Kassina," whose beautiful bubbling sounds surrounded us. On the way back to camp, it began to rain. Bugs that were so big they looked unreal pelted us in the face. I pulled my tan safari hat down on my head and pulled the hood on my rain jacket over the hat. A large beetle struck my cheekbone so hard it left a red splotch. It stung like a literal smack in the face, a wake-up call. I was alive, I was present, I was laughing. My anxiety had melted away. I was immensely grateful to be there at that moment, pelted by bugs and rain.

Back at camp, Marius and Nicolaas joined us for dinner and shared more fascinating stories. I sat on the edge of my seat, captivated by their lives, which were so different from mine. It continued to pound rain all night long.

The next day, Marius took us to Sand River. I felt even more at ease after learning he had spent weeks alone in the bush, building his own shelter, catching and cooking his own food—all survivalist aspects of his guide training.

At the Sand River, we watched the rainwater as it trickled down from nearby mountains and made its way to the dry riverbed. Before long, the rivulets became a stream and the water began to gush, expanding from bank to bank. It was like witnessing the birth of a flood—peace and silence on one side, the fast and violent crashing of water on the other. It spread far and wide, covering small islands of sand, brush and trees, washing over all that was beneath it. As I took in the sight, I considered how simple it was to begin again. In nature, there was a fresh start in every moment, every day. There was something to appreciate in each new beginning. There was no need to dwell on the past or to think too much about the future. Honoring nature was about being present in the here and now.

As our journey continued, a herd of five elephants stomped their giant feet slowly toward us, and an adorable baby followed behind, its tail flailing in all directions. I locked eyes with the patriarch's deep, soulful eyes. He walked past with a swagger that suggested he could snuff me out in a heartbeat, and my inclination was to panic. But I also felt a deep connection to him. Marius assured us the herd would walk past and continue on its way. He said most animals saw the safari Jeep as part of the landscape and paid little attention to the vehicles or the humans in them.

Later, we saw a second herd of elephants with a baby. They poked their trunks into the sandy riverbed, drew water up from beneath the ground, and poured it into their mouths. They sprayed each other playfully, like kids running through a twisty sprinkler on a hot summer day. The female elephant laid down on her side, totally relaxed, just a mama taking a break from playing with her children.

Throughout our time at the reserve, we saw giraffes, zebras, waterbuck and many beautiful birds. My favorite was the Lilac-breasted Roller; it was covered with beautiful feathers of light purple and turquoise on its tummy, and had bright red cheeks, and turquoise and deep blue and orange wings.

In the afternoons, from our hotel window, I watched baboons playfully climbing trees, swinging gracefully from one to another. I marveled at how they showed affection and cared for each other, sitting together and grooming one another. I could have spent hours watching them, trying to understand their social systems and complexities.

One evening, a lightning storm in the distance

painted the entire sky with color. As the rain showered my face, I inhaled the scent and taste of the freshest rainwater I'd ever encountered. It reminded me of my days as a kid at summer sleep-away camp, when we would go puddle jumping in the rain.

On our final morning at the Mala Mala Reserve, I felt a little heartbroken. While the next stop on our journey was Tswalu, a wildlife reserve in the Kalahari Desert, I didn't want to leave this magical place. For our final ride, all the kids went with Marius, and the adults rode with Nicolaas. I noticed the difference in my body from the first day to the last. I was more relaxed. My breath flowed freely as I took in the exquisite morning. An hour into the bush, we stopped near a lion eating his bloody kill. I couldn't take my eyes off the gruesome sight. Over the past five days, I had learned so much about lions and their dens; their family dynamics were not unlike those of human families.

Every moment in the bush, I felt like I was exactly where I needed to be. I felt inspired. I felt renewed. I felt invigorated. I felt alive. The song "On Top of the World" by Imagine Dragons played in repeat in my head. This trip had reawakened my soul. It reminded me how crucial education, travel and being in nature was to my being. I imagined what it would be like to move to Africa and live off the land. I never wanted to leave. For the first time in years, I'd found contentment in the present—I wanted to hold it tight and never let it go. I wasn't sure when or where I had lost that feeling of appreciating each moment, but I knew that once I was home, I needed to figure out a way to feel it again in my daily life. In Setswana, a Bantu language spoken by South Africans, "tswalu" means a new beginning. Maybe this was my tswalu.

As we headed back to camp to say our goodbyes, we crossed the airstrip just in time to see a beautiful male leopard. He slinked lazily toward our car. As he came closer, I realized he was stalking something in the distance.

"A wildebeest," Nicolaas said, at barely a whisper.

Before I could draw my next breath, the leopard gracefully disappeared into the tall grass. I wondered the significance of a leopard greeting us on our first day, and another bidding us goodbye on our last.

The place of true healing is a fierce place ... of monstrous beauty and endless dark and glimmering light. And you have to work really, really, really hard to get there.
—CHERYL STRAYED

I first noticed a shift in my mom after my nephew died. The joy that had once been in her beautiful, chocolate brown eyes had faded. A few years after that, she sustained a bad concussion during a bicycling accident. As a result, she experienced memory loss and became fearful and anxious. Her happiness was replaced by negativity. Her body recovered, but her brain was not the same. One minute, she was critical of something I said or did, and the next she would praise me for being the best daughter. It was hard to navigate, like living with Jekyll and Hyde—I never knew who I was going to get.

I missed my strong, glamorous mother. The one who taught aerobics in the '80s and was approached by a local cable television station to host her own show. To prepare for the gig, she flew to Los Angeles and took classes from Richard Simmons and Jane

Fonda. She came home with brightly colored leotards and tights, skinny belts, and thick, scrunchy legwarmers. She brought the Los Angeles vibe back to Minneapolis. I didn't realize how much happiness her TV show, "Firm Up with Elaine," had brought her until years later.

"Those were the best days of my life," she had said. "I was my best self—alive and happy."

I wished I could help her find her way back to that same kind of joy. I suggested a daily gratitude practice. I gave her journals with prompts to write in. I suggested she focus on the things that brought her joy. She would try something for a while, and her interest would quickly fizzle. I realized I could be kind and empathetic, but I could not change her mindset. Only she could do that.

In 2017, five years after her concussion, Mom called me from California on a Friday afternoon. I had a sixth sense something was wrong—I felt it deep in my bones. As she explained she was at the hospital for a second ultrasound (she hadn't told me about the first), my heart began to race. I sat anchored in my kitchen, staring out the window as snowflakes floated softly to the ground. I clutched the phone tightly as she shared the news no one wants to hear: the scan revealed my mother had breast cancer.

I couldn't fathom how this could be. Physically, she was a picture of health. She worked out, ate well and took care of herself.

Suddenly, it felt like there were a million miles between us. I wanted to jump onto a plane immediately to see her, to hug her and tell her it was going to be OK. I wanted to take control of the situation, talk to the doctors.

Mom cried and cried, and I cried with her. I worried she might not have the will to fight. I wouldn't allow my mind to go down the dark roads it sometimes traveled. I focused on the future, the good times that were surely yet to come.

After the shock of the news wore off, I noticed a shift. A fire had returned to Mom's eyes for the first time in years. She would face cancer head-on with everything she had. The strength I remembered her possessing when I was a teen returned in full force. My mom was back with a purpose.

As the cancer treatment began, her doctors seemed to poo-poo anything even remotely alternative I read about or mentioned to support her healing journey, including simple suggestions like eating a rainbow of fresh fruits and vegetables to nourish her body.

"Don't worry about healthy food," her well-respected doctor said dismissively. "You need the calories—eat all the bagels and donuts you want."

In my mind, I rolled my eyes.

Frustrated and convinced incorporating alternative therapies into her cancer treatment regimen could be helpful, I spent hours searching for answers online and reading books. The process gave me a sense of hope when I felt helpless. I was determined to find all the possible ways she could take control of managing the disease, thinking it might remove some of her fear surrounding cancer. I began bombarding her with information and gave her a dense book that detailed what she could be doing to help herself.

Though my efforts were well-intended, I overwhelmed her. She was deep into her treatment and had developed "chemo brain"—a term used to describe thinking and memory problems patients with cancer often experience before, during or after chemotherapy. She couldn't process what she was reading, nor could she think beyond the regimen her doctor had prescribed.

In those early days of my mom's cancer treatment, I noticed that my mom, my dad, Louie and I felt closer again. We were connected in ways we hadn't been since my dad first got sober. Every week, we spent time together, huddled around Mom for hours as powerful chemicals coursed through her veins, poisoning the fast-growing cells in her body. We would have long conversations about the things we would do when this was behind us; we all imagined better days. My mom longed for spa vacations and wanted to get away. My dad talked about buying an RV and driving across the country. I couldn't imagine my parents actually doing this, but their daydreaming about it gave me hope. I hadn't felt so connected to my brother since he was in college. Our relationship was strengthened through our mother's cancer journey, and I was grateful for it.

Despite my mom's inability to process the information I shared about an integrative approach to cancer treatment, I continued to learn as much as I could. Instead of bombarding her with information, I shared it in bits and pieces. One morning, as I sat with her and held her hand during one of her chemo infusions, I gave snippets of something I'd recently read.

"Marnie," she said, looking directly at me, her eyes filled with sadness. "No matter how much you want to help, you just can't understand what I am going through." My heart tore in two. "And I hope you never ever have to," she added.

Maybe I couldn't give my mom the kind of help I wanted to, but I could continue to help in more practical ways—by being present during her weekly chemo appointments, and by lending an ear when she needed someone to talk to. My parents assumed I would do these things, that I would be a dutiful daughter, and I wanted to do whatever I could to help Mom get through such a difficult time.

It wasn't easy to drop my three kids at school, to put my two businesses and other obligations aside and speed to her appointments to make sure I was on time. I often parked in a spot across the street from the hospital with limited hours so I could race in and out; each time I hoped there wouldn't be a ticket on my car when I returned. It wasn't easy to be there for Mom while also schlepping my kids to and from activities, shopping, cooking meals and managing a household. I was often exhausted and overwhelmed, and juggling it all was a challenge. Louie seemed unfazed, casually sauntering into the cancer center at the exact right moment and saying the thing Mom most wanted to hear.

I did my best to be positive, even when I didn't feel that way inside. When Mom mentioned that all the negative information and sad cancer stories were bringing her down, an idea bubbled up. I couldn't understand exactly what she was going through, but there were many women who had their own cancer journeys, survivors and thrivers whose experiences could provide inspiration and guidance to women like my mom. I could connect with these women, hear their stories, gain knowledge from what they shared, and pass it along to my mom and women like her, so they would not feel so alone.

I made a list of women I knew who had experienced cancer. I asked my network for referrals. I let friends and family on social media know my mom had breast cancer and I was collecting positive stories from women of all ages who'd overcome cancer.

Over the course of six months, I conducted and recorded 30 in-depth interviews with amazing, strong, thriving women. Each story was unique. All of them dealt with their trauma in different ways.

For some survivors, I was the first person they shared their entire story with. Some women wanted to put what they'd endured behind them and move on. Others wanted to share their knowledge by doing cancer-related nonprofit work. One woman's husband wrote a book about his experience as a male spouse supporting his wife through cancer—a perspective I hadn't thought much about before that.

I cried with each story and developed a kinship with the women. I planned to compile the stories and publish them in a book with alternative health and wellness tips. While that book did not come to be, I am eternally grateful to those women. They gave me hope for a bright future with my mom.

Throughout Mom's time at the cancer center, my family and I had watched many other oncology patients participate in the "last day of chemo" ritual of ringing the bell. After 18 long months, it was finally my mom's turn. Dad brought doughnuts for the staff who'd loved and cared for her over the past year and a half. We all gathered around to cheer her on as she rang the bell. She was exhausted and hopeful, and most importantly, she had made it.

You wanna fly, you got to give up the shit that weighs you down.
—TONI MORRISON

I never liked clutter. Even as a little girl, I kept my bedroom neat and organized. Every few months, I sorted through my clothing and trinkets. I'd have a mini garage sale on an old card table that I'd set up in our driveway, or I would donate the items to charity.

My parents were not emotional about material items. I was awed by how easily they placed things straight into the garbage bin or donation pile. They're still like this today. Once they're done with something, out of the house it goes. There are a few items I have trouble parting with—photographs, journals, jewelry, my kids' artwork. I have bins full of their masterpieces in our basement furnace room, stored away to be appreciated again someday.

In 2017, I began studying under a naturopath named Dr. Stephen Cabral. I had been listening to his podcast, "The Cabral Concept," and his teachings on nutrition, sleep, stress, supplements and mindset resonated with me. I enrolled in his very first class for integrative health practitioners, which would build on what I had learned during my training from IIN.

Dr. Cabral explained the human body in a way that really made sense to me. I began to truly understand the digestive process, and I could actually picture a piece of food as it made its way from the mouth and traveled all the way through the body until it was expelled. I even learned about healthy poop and how it should look.

I also learned about lab testing from Dr. Cabral. I lab tested myself, and confirmed I had dairy and gluten sensitivities. I discovered my cortisol levels were higher than ideal. I learned I would benefit from adding vitamin B, zinc, omegas and other supplements to my daily routine.

My family did lab tests as well. The kids learned that cutting dairy and gluten might make them feel better, which they weren't quite ready to hear. I hoped they would eventually use the information to see if it did in fact make them feel better. In the meantime, I got them started taking vitamin D regularly, to help their bodies absorb and retain calcium, build bone, combat infection, and reduce inflammation, depression and cancer cell growth.

My training with Dr. Cabral led to a major

decluttering at home. I cleaned out the entire pantry. I cleaned out the fridge. I reorganized fruits, veggies and raw nuts in glass jars so they wouldn't be exposed to the toxins in plastic containers. I placed the cilantro in water in a canning jar in the fridge where it lasted for weeks instead of days. Each week, I spent time unpacking groceries and methodically placing everything on the shelves, which I had labeled with categories like protein, avocados, leftovers and dairy. I threw out the foods and snacks that had no nutritional value or were total crap and kept a small amount of higher quality processed snacks.

I posted photos of my beautifully organized refrigerator on Instagram. I followed professional organizers who inspired me like Michele Vig of @neatlittlenest, who had written a book called "The Holistic Guide to Decluttering," and Elsa Elbert of @composed_living. When my kids asked where all the good snacks had gone, I explained we were making changes.

"Strive to eat a rainbow each day!" I'd say as they looked at each other and rolled their eyes.

I read hundreds of online reviews about kitchen organization tools. I alphabetized the spices. I labeled the pantry shelves, so everyone knew where items belonged. I got rid of utensils that were melted or worn out, Teflon pans we had received years ago as a wedding gift, an ice cream maker we never used. Once I completed the kitchen, I was inspired, motivated and ready for more. The lack of clutter was a release for me. The more organized things were, the less messy I felt inside. Off to the next room I went.

I spent hours organizing the bathroom. I learned about the Environmental Working Group (EWG), a company that rates products for safety based on ingredients, and realized my drawers and shelves were filled with products containing harsh chemicals and fragrances that could disrupt hormones and cause skin irritation. I discovered the Think Dirty app, which rates beauty products based on ingredients— those with higher amounts of toxins have higher scores. I kept only products with a score of three or lower.

"Time to toss the toxins!" I declared.

My daughter Sage was inspired as well.

"Guess what, mom?" she announced. "I got my bathroom shelf down to a one!"

She went on to help a close friend toss the toxins as well. Soon after, as the editor-in-chief of her high school newspaper, Sage wrote an article on clean beauty and the importance of using nontoxic products. I was so proud. I began noticing small ripples spreading from the changes I was making at home.

Sage helped me tackle my bedroom closet, which involved trying on just about everything. This was a daunting task after months of living in Lululemon pants and tank tops imprinted with inspirational sayings.

As I tried on items and consulted Sage for fashion advice, she would laugh.

"Mom, that is so out of style," she said again and again.

I adopted the Marie Kondo method of asking myself if the item brought me joy. I took it a step further and asked, "Do I feel sexy in this?" "Do I feel confident?" If not, into the giant black plastic donation bag it went.

I unearthed a powder blue leather jacket with several zippered pockets, reminiscent of an '80s-style jacket. I had splurged on it years earlier when my friend Nicole and I spent an afternoon shopping at a few high-end boutiques in the North Loop that I rarely frequented, and only with her or my mom. On that day, it felt like we were starring in the movie "Pretty Woman." The store manager, Tony, with his impeccable style and long, sleek ponytail, pulled together outfit after outfit for us to try on.

"This would look fabulous on you!" he said. "If you pair it with these heels—unbelievable!" I lost count of how many times he said "Gorgeous!"

Tony knew all the right things to say, and we got swirled up in the moment. I came home with several items that were out of my budget. The jacket seemed so chic and sophisticated in the store, but whenever I tried it on at home, I felt ridiculous. So there it was in my closet, never worn.

"Mom, this jacket is SO cool!" Sage said the moment she spotted it. "Why don't you ever wear it?"

"I look silly in it," I said matter-of-factly. "Powder blue leather, I don't know what I was thinking."

"The '80s are back!" she exclaimed. "I can't believe the tags are still on it!"

"Do you want it?" I asked her, thinking back to my mom passing along outfits of hers that I admired.

"Seriously, Mom?" Sage asked, trying to contain her excitement.

"It's all yours," I said, imagining how much cuter it would look on her 17-year-old figure. "And if I ever want to wear it, I'll borrow it from you."

As we continued to declutter my collection of clothing, I identified several items I wore repeatedly. I wondered why I'd let all the other items in my closet collect dust when they could bring joy to someone else. Initially, I felt guilty placing some pieces in the giveaway bag. But once they were out of sight, I felt lighter. I never thought about them again. I committed to carefully considering each future purchase before pulling the trigger. I would call it mindful purchasing.

Clearing the clutter in my mind was a different story. The voice inside my head had a running commentary, and it wasn't always so nice. It lived in the past, telling and retelling old stories repeatedly. It fretted about the future and potential problems, like what cabin my daughter would be assigned at sleep-away camp and whether she'd be with her friends. I focused on issues out of my control.

During yoga training, I learned I could not control anything outside of myself. For a Type A person like me, it was an important lesson and took daily practice and self-talk. I was often surrounded by people who liked to be in control. I had to learn to retrain my brain to live in the moment. That meant focusing inward and creating the life I wanted for myself. I discovered that when I was absorbed in something I loved, I lived in the moment. When I felt content, I lived in the moment. Still, every so often, the clutter in my mind would continue to creep in and get in the way.

As I continued the process of interviewing and recording the stories of cancer survivors I'd started during my mom's cancer journey, a phone conversation with my aunt Elaine, who is married to my dad's brother Daniel ("Nooper" as we all call him) had a profound effect on me. Aunt Elaine had overcome breast cancer five years before my mom and shared a mindful visualization she used to help clear her body of the cancer, similar to the way an athlete envisions a perfect race or victorious finish.

"I began to picture a little man, a janitor in my closet, who cleaned each organ in my body," she said, animatedly. "He'd say, 'OK, time for the kidneys and the liver!' and put them in the washer and then the dryer. I visualized my clean liver and kidneys and the little man putting them back into my body. I visualized this cleaning process with all my organs, any part of my body that hurt. I imagined the little man scrubbing and ridding my body of any cancer that might be lurking. I pictured him walking around my breast with a magnifying glass and a little cleaning tool. Sometimes he would focus on my brain. If something was not quite right, he would fix it. And then back into the closet he went." I felt the electricity of Aunt Elaine's positive energy coming through the phone. "Even now, he cleans my organs every single day."

Her body's own personal cleaning man. It was perfect! I had a powerful realization: only I could clear the clutter in my mind.

In my yoga teacher training, one of my instructors had directed our group to imagine that nagging, nay-saying internal voice as a little person on your shoulder, the one that maliciously chimed into your ear: "You are not good enough," "You are not smart enough," "You are not pretty enough," "You can't do that." She suggested one way to address it was literally flicking that imaginary person off your shoulder, and even telling it, "Get out of my life!"

I laughed as I sat cross-legged on my purple yoga mat and imagined it. But it made a lot of sense. I never spoke to others the way my negative internal voice spoke to me. I began calling that voice Flick, and whenever it came out, I'd cast it off.

My aunt Elaine's approach resonated with me as well. So in addition to flicking away the negative shit, I would enlist the help of my own personal cleaning man—someone who would give gentle reminders when there was too much clutter in my head and treat me with loving kindness.

I worked on being more present in my everyday life. I longed to feel present and alive in my home environment, even while surrounded by daily stressors. I had discovered that travels like my African adventure set my soul on fire. The key, I realized, was nature. It had always been the solution for this, though I hadn't always been conscious of its powerful effect on me.

The Minneapolis suburb where I grew up was surrounded by 90 miles of biking, running and walking trails. The trail nearest our house meandered through the woods with bridges and a bubbling creek. I would ride my bicycle to Dairy Queen on those trails on hot summer days. I spent lazy summer afternoons exploring miles of paths with neighborhood kids. Once, my friends and I waded in the creek and when we got out, we all had leeches on our ankles and calves. I never set foot in it again. Aside from the leeches, being in nature brought me a sense of peace.

I learned to ski in Northern Minnesota when I was 3 years old. I donned a Snoopy hat and a royal blue snowsuit belted at the waist. My dad held me upright between his legs as we skied together down the hill. I loved it from the get-go. The exhilaration of the cold wind in my face, the invincible feeling as I bombed the hill in a pizza wedge. I became a less aggressive skier as an adult. Still, swooshing down a hill or mountain, soft powder beneath me, gorgeous peaks surrounding me—I could truly be in the moment. I could focus only on the path in front of me. Mindful skiing.

I would experience a similar feeling during winter walks. Whenever my stress would begin to mount, or after I'd been sitting in front of the computer too long, I'd heed nature's call. It could be 10 degrees below zero outside with an arctic sun blazing in the sky. There could be mounds of snow piled high along the edges of the streets where the plow has cleared a path. I would layer on long underwear, wool socks, a snowflake ski sweater that reminded me of the mountains, bulky snow pants, a neck gator and a puffy coat down to my ankles—my dog-walking coat. "Not very cute," Baubie would say, but very practical. I would pull a hat on so low and the gator up so high that only my eyes were visible. I'd bundle up our dog Lila in her plaid fleece coat, and she'd begin to prance because she knew what it meant: "I am going on an adventure with Mom!"

As Lila and I trekked the trail, I would appreciate how peaceful it was with just the sound of snow crunching under my boots. We would walk and walk, breathing in the fresh, crisp air. I would take in the smell of the pine trees and picture the air entering my nostrils, my nose hairs freezing into tiny icicles. Sometimes, I would spot a deer and it would look me straight in the eye before darting deep into the woods. Or I would hear a winter bird that hadn't flown south whistling a pretty tune. I would let go of my to-do list for an hour or so.

Nature walks continue to be a daily practice for Lila and me all year long. Come rain, or snow, sleet or hail, we never miss a walk. Some of my favorite moments are during the winter, when Lila runs off-leash. It is against city rules, but on the days when it is so frigid that not another soul is on the trail, I am a rule breaker. Lila tears around in pure bliss, running ahead and then circling back before she gets too far, her sparkly green eyes looking and waiting for me. In these moments, I feel as free as I imagine she does. I experience all my senses and tune into myself. Mostly, I focus on the moment. But every now and then, I asked the universe for help with something.

For years I thought about creating a sacred space for meditation at home but did not consider myself a great mediator. When not in nature, I struggled to focus, to stop my mind from wandering, to keep myself from falling asleep or fidgeting—to find stillness. I finally enrolled in meditation teacher training so I could improve my skills to help myself and my clients. And during warm summer nights, while my family sat outside having dinner on the deck surrounded by the chirping of crickets, I practiced meditation in my newly appointed space upstairs.

I set up an area for a puja table—a decorative tray table that holds sacred offerings to a deity (in my case to the universe)—on a maple cabinet that once held toys my kids had outgrown. I'd found a puja of dark wood with an intricate patchwork design on the top and wavy legs.

On top of the puja, I placed a mini wooden altar. On the altar, I placed a Buddha, which had been given to me by my dad. Years earlier, he had made the first of what would become his annual trip to Bangkok. Knowing my appreciation of Eastern philosophy, he brought back a Buddha, and it became the start of my collection. I appreciated the teeny Buddhas with intricate details most, but my collection has grown to many in all shapes and sizes. The Buddha I placed on the altar was golden in color and two inches tall.

Next I added to the puja a red and gold satin pillow that held a singing bowl. When struck or circled with a mallet, the sounds and vibrations of a singing bowl promote relaxation in the body and brain. I'd picked out this one after I experienced the powerful effects of a singing bowl during yoga teacher training. (I would realize later I hadn't considered that someone else would need to be present to strike the bowl while I meditated.)

In the center of my puja, I placed a rectangular lime green candle containing a prosperity symbol that my mother had given me, palo santo wood given to me by my massage therapist, which is used to purify air, dispel evil spirits and cleanse negative energy, three books of matches from my travels, and a purple glass heart from a dear friend.

The last and most important item on my table was a 1-by-1-inch "Be Happy" book Sage gave me when she was 15. She had cut the tiny pages from soft, white paper napkins and stapled them together in the most perfect way. Each page featured one thing a person could do to be happy: Dance freely! Watch a funny movie! It was like the small, self-help books on display at the check-out counter at Barnes and Noble, only a million times better because it came from my creative and thoughtful daughter.

Next to my puja, I placed a larger silver Buddha who gazed over the room. His expression was one of extreme peace and tranquility, yet I felt his strength in his tall, relaxed posture. I was finally ready to meditate.

The traditional way to meditate is sitting upright in a cross-legged position, but in my new meditation space, I discovered a position where I could still stay focused without falling fast asleep like I would in savasana, or corpse pose. I chose "legs up the wall pose" or viparita karani, a favorite posture of mine. As my body and back released, I succumbed to an other-worldly state. I felt as if I were floating here, there and nowhere, my hands and arms heavy at my sides. I would think about energy, and the flow or life force that moved through my body.

Each time I meditated, I would I lie in this position, lights off, candles lit, the soothing voice of whatever guide I had chosen for that day playing on my smartphone. I would surrender every cell of my body, breathing methodically, moving the stagnant clutter out of my mind, and releasing it from my body. I thought about time in nature—an intense hike at Arches National Park, miles away from civilization, sucking water from my Camelbak straw. I recalled the feeling of the water replenishing and circulating energy and life into my cells.

If my mind wandered, if I began thinking about what it may have been like for adventurers long ago who discovered the various places in nature I visited, I would tell myself to stay with my breath. I would bring my mind back to the present. It was an ongoing process to stay present.

As I continued to work on decluttering my physical surroundings and thoughts in my head, I also continued to let go of relationships that did not serve me well. This process had started years ago, after the botched girls' trip with the moms from my kids' school. It felt good to be free of the toxicity of those relationships, and now I was getting clear on the relationships that deserved my energy in the first place. The more I tuned into my gut, the more content I felt.

.

**Only those who risk going too far
can possibly find out how far one can go.
—T.S. ELIOT**

Jordan was a literal brain thinker; every decision he made was backed by studies, evidence and proof. I preferred to ask the universe: "Please help me figure this out." And it was working. I had learned to dig deep, trust my instincts, and believe the answers existed within me. My gut was rarely, if ever wrong.

In 2017, my friend Julie prepared to launch her business, ModernWell, a women's coworking space and community. Before it officially opened, she gave me a tour. The space was flooded with bright and natural light from floor-to-ceiling windows. There were zones for working together or quietly. The décor was Zen-infused with clean lines, white furniture, large green plants and artwork created by local women. Inspirational sayings like, "Supporting another person's success won't dampen your own," and "Collaboration over competition" adorned the walls and added to its warm and welcoming vibe.

ModernWell was already attracting a wide range of professional women. I had been working from home for many years, which at times felt a bit lonely and isolating. I wasn't sure about investing in a founding membership, but my gut was telling me it could be good to get out of the house a few days a week. After the tour and learning more about Julie's vision and passion for building a community of women working together, I was sold.

The negative voice in my head began to nag. My business was small, and my health coaching career was in its infancy. How would I compare to the other members? What if I wasn't good enough? I used my tools to silence that voice and work through my fears.

A few weeks into my membership, I was still unsure of myself as I walked through the door, but the space was so welcoming and calming that I continued to go. I would casually chat with people I knew, and they would introduce me to others I didn't know.

Months later, on a sunny fall day, Julie approached me with a smile. We had chatted numerous times about my businesses and the various directions I considered taking them.

"There's an amazing woman here named Jasna, who leads a business mastermind," she said. "She asked if I'd like to gift someone a spot in the group—would you like to be that person?"

I enthusiastically took her up on the offer.

Jasna's program consisted of five in-person sessions, each three hours long, and they were held in ModernWell's bright, beautiful conference room. On the day of the first session, I looked around the table at the 11 other hip women in the group and wondered if my casual jeans and cute top were too mom-ish. I focused instead on the words of encouragement written on the notebooks placed in front of each of us with a pen, a breath mint and chocolates, and a gemstone. Mine was purple, one of my favorite colors.

I introduced myself to the woman beside me, Stephanie. "What do you do?" I asked casually, feeling a bit nervous.

"I'm a holistic health coach," she said, looking relaxed in her chair.

"Really?" I asked, blown away that I had chosen to sit right next to the one other person in the room who did exactly what I was doing. "Me too!"

The more we talked, the more we discovered we had in common. When it was time for formal introductions, I wondered how I felt about being in a business mastermind with someone whose business was so similar. I reminded myself of Julie's vision for ModernWell: collaboration over competition. Women supporting women.

Jasna was both stunning and commanding as she addressed the group. Her hair was long and dark, her eyes were piercing blue and kind. She wore a cherry red dress and black studded heels. She was just the right mix of warm and professional. She explained that the sessions would each focus on different themes such as entrepreneurship, sales, marketing and thriving in our personal lives. We would build relationships with other women in the group and support one another in our journeys. The last session would include a lifestyle photo shoot, and each of us would receive copies of the images to market our businesses.

Every week I felt closer to the women in the group. We were all from different backgrounds and all of us were working to start or grow our businesses. We had our own struggles, but collectively we solved problems and influenced each other in positive ways.

One afternoon, about halfway through a session, I approached Stephanie with an idea.

"Do you have any interest in running health coaching groups together?" I asked. "Instead of competing for clients, we could team up."

I could almost see the wheels in her mind spinning as I posed the question. Within a month of that conversation, we hosted our first multi-session group wellness program at ModernWell. It was wonderful to be part of a team after working solo for so long. We worked well together and learned we had much more in common than our chosen professions. We were both Aries, born two days apart (I was one year older). We each had three kids around the same ages. We had both lived in another country for a number of years. We had traveled to many of the same places.

We had some differences as well. While we both lived in Minneapolis suburbs, she was in Edina, and I was in Minnetonka. Though we had ModernWell in common, we had no mutual friends outside the coworking space and lived in completely different worlds. Stephanie introduced me to a lot of new people, and I did the same for her. I loved this aspect of our relationship.

After the success of our first group wellness program, we decided to continue working together. We created workshops focused on sugar and gut health. We attended in-person conferences together, often to promote our products and programs.

ModernWell, and the relationships I was building

there, showed me I could thrive outside of my comfort zone. When I heard another member was seeking guests for her "Women Inspired!" podcast, and the idea felt scary to me, I took it as a sign it was something worth pursuing. I connected with the host to let her know I was interested.

During the recorded interview, she asked questions about my businesses and life, and how I juggled it all. Responses seemed to flow from me like a river. I was surprised by how much I enjoyed the process and how easy it was. Something inside me was unleashed. I knew immediately that I wanted to start a podcast. I had majored in journalism in college, after all. Perhaps this was a full circle moment.

"Do you want to cohost a podcast?" I eagerly asked Stephanie, sitting on the edge of my seat. By this time, we were meeting regularly to plan workshops and create materials.

I hoped she didn't think I was totally nuts. In addition to health coaching, I was teaching YogaCalm® a half-day every week for elementary students at a local public school. Plus, my promotional products business, ChillyBean, was busier than ever.

"Maybe …" Stephanie said with a smile, giving me just the right amount of hope.

"We could interview health and wellness experts,

including each other, and drop a new episode each week," I said excitedly. "Just think of how many people we could reach! With a podcast, we could teach health and wellness to people all around the world!"

A short time later, "The Art of Living Well Podcast" was born. We released the first episode, an introduction to the two of us and our backgrounds, on Oct. 30, 2019.

During that first episode, we read from scripts word-for-word. I cringed when I heard my scratchy-sounding recorded voice. It reminded me of the voice of the little girl my dad affectionately referred to as "The Rasp." I listened to other programs and studied other host's styles to figure out what I liked and didn't like. The learning curve for podcasting was steep. By the third episode of "The Art of Living Well Podcast," my voice was much more relaxed. I discovered that I sounded better without a script. I had never been comfortable speaking off the cuff— but soon I was bantering with Stephanie and our guests with ease as we recorded. I was so proud of myself.

The podcast was feeding a new passion I didn't know existed. From booking guests, to recording, editing and marketing, the entire process was a challenge. Stephanie and I were committed to doing everything on our own so we could understand all aspects of podcasting. We also wanted to save money (we were operating on a shoestring budget in those early days) and hoped to grow it organically, by word of mouth.

From the start, one of my favorite parts was researching guests and subjects to be featured. I would eagerly jump down the rabbit hole of each guest's life, knowledge and experience. I would read and listen to articles and interviews and compose questions to keep listeners engaged. Often, our guests were authors, and I loved the perk of getting an advance copy of their book to read before the interview. I was inspired by their stories, and I believed everyone had something interesting to share with the world.

I didn't realize just how much I would learn from our guests each week. We would dive deeply into topics like digital wellness, sex and intimacy, sobriety, finding joy, micro-dosing and so much more. I felt like a sponge soaking up advice and knowledge. At the end of our conversations, we would ask guests, "What does the art of living well mean to you?"

One guest, Michele Vig, said, "The art of

living well for me is living a life that is true to your soul's call."

Another guest, Michelle Olson said, "The art of living well means to live authentically present in every moment."

And guest Meg Hirshberg said, "Living well is learning to live with imperfection and celebrating that imperfection."

There were so many great nuggets in each conversation. Oftentimes, even after we recorded an episode, I was inspired to continue learning about the topic. At the dinner table, I'd often share my excitement about how amazing a guest had been that day. The kids would ask questions, inspired by my enthusiasm and interested in learning more. Jordan did too, sometimes challenging a guest's point of view from a Western medicine perspective.

It wasn't all smooth sailing. Parts of podcasting were hard and time-consuming. There was always more that could be done. But I didn't mind all the hours spent creating graphics in Canva, or tinkering on an episode in Garageband until it was perfectly edited. I was doing fulfilling work and it lit me up. I felt like I was glowing from the inside out.

Something else happened during this time. For years I had been developing my voice as a writer and storyteller. What had started as a slow simmer was now beginning to bubble and explode as a podcast host. I enrolled in a public speaking course to help hone my skills. Perhaps part of me was still trying to prove to my parents (and to the rest of the world) that what I had to say was important. Or perhaps I just really enjoyed learning and being a student.

In early 2020, when the pandemic hit, rather than meeting in person as we'd done previously, Stephanie and I began recording our podcasts from home via Zoom. We would meet in the morning in our PJs, sweats or workout clothes. There was nowhere else to be, no shuttling kids to soccer, dance or piano lessons. We hashed out our goals for the podcast and our partnership. We worked on our podcasting skills, which entailed perfecting our processes and hiring a professional editor. The dedicated time allowed me to focus on my business and give it the attention it deserved.

I was also enjoying the time at home with my three kids, who were then 19, 17 and 14 years old, and seeing more of Jordan, who was no longer working long hours in direct patient care. He was much more relaxed in his sweatpants and slippers, which he paired with a white dress shirt, tie and sport coat whenever he needed to present to an audience or host an important meeting online. There was nowhere to go, nowhere to be, and for my family, it felt like a precious gift.

When the weight of the world outside our COVID bubble felt heavy, I took long walks in the woods and around my neighborhood. I thought about hiking trips I'd taken in the past, and the huge impact both traveling and nature had had on my life.

I recalled when Jordan and I had visited the Grand Tetons, pushing each other mile after mile on the Cascade Canyon Trail, one of the most spectacular trails I had ever been on. We took a ferry across Jenny Lake and journeyed on the 10-mile out-and-back, surrounded by rushing waters from glacial runoff, gorgeous cliffs and wildflowers in deep purples and yellows. It was magical. Until an old injury of Jordan's flared up and we ended up having to turn back early. This tested my patience—I wanted to finish what I started and complete the miles. I reminded myself to focus on the exquisiteness of nature and live in the moment. It was about the journey, not the destination.

I thought about another time years earlier, visiting Lake Tahoe, where Jordan and I hiked five miles to a waterfall on the Tahoe Rim Trail. I convinced him to push further on, to the Mount Rose Summit. The beauty was spectacular—wildflowers covered the ground like a blanket in a rainbow of colors. We walked on obscure paths through babbling brooks and trudged through patches of snow to the 10,500-foot summit with unbelievable views in all directions— our reward for completing the challenge. I hadn't thought about the hike back down. We hadn't packed enough water and food for a longer excursion. Jordan was furious with me for pushing us to the peak while he battled altitude sickness. As the sun dipped down to the horizon, we finally crossed paths with another couple who spoke no English but pointed us in the right direction using the satellite map on their phone. Eight hours and more than 40,000 steps from where we began, we made it back to our car, delirious from lack of water. Despite Jordan's altitude sickness it was a magical day, and we agreed we would do it again. We also learned what we would do differently: download maps beforehand; plan our route ahead of time; always bring extra food and water; reapply sunscreen often; and most importantly, acclimate our bodies to the altitude before a strenuous climb. I will never forget the hikers who pointed us in the right direction that day.

When the pandemic first hit and gave no signs of letting up, I knew it might be a while before we would travel again, so I focused on the nature outside my back door. I focused on the strong and resilient person I was becoming.

**A thankful heart is not only the greatest
virtue, but the parent of all the other virtues.
—CICERO**

It was a stunning 75-degree fall day. The sun was bright and happy; the wind was warm. I had exercised early in the morning and noticed how strong I felt, how good I looked as I checked my reflection in the mirrored wall of my basement home gym.

As I sat at the desk in my home office working, I was occasionally distracted by the walkers zipping past my large street-facing window. They all seemed to be enjoying the weather.

When it was time for lunch, I tossed together a salad using fresh bell peppers, carrots, tomatoes, cucumbers, hearts of palm and other veggies I had chopped and organized in the fridge earlier in the week. I sat at the table outside on my deck and ate, enjoying the heat of the sun on my back. In between bites, I caught up on social media, liking and commenting on "Class of 2022 Senior Parent

Challenge" posts featuring parents' favorite photos of their soon-to-graduate high school seniors.

After lunch, I headed to my annual mammogram. Just another item to check off my to-do list. I'd be in and out of there in no time and on with my day.

I walked into the clinic, sunglasses perched casually on the top of my head, and checked in. I noticed a woman close to my age sitting in the waiting area. Her pale, gaunt face was accentuated by a brightly colored scarf wrapped around her head, and her shoulders sagged. I smiled briefly in compassion, grateful my visit was for a routine exam. Before I had a chance to sit down, an assistant peeked around the door and called my name. I hurried in after her and quickly changed into a gown.

As I took a seat in the second waiting room, holding the robe together over my chest, I felt my heart begin to thud. "Deep breaths," I coached myself. "You have nothing to worry about."

"That's what your mom and aunt Elaine thought, too," Flick said.

"Their cancers weren't genetic," I replied, launching him off my shoulder.

I picked up the copy of "Real Simple" magazine and flipped mindlessly through the pages until my name was called again. I followed the chipper, chatty technician down the hall and into the cold exam room. I'd had many mammograms and was accustomed to having my breasts smashed, prodded and poked.

"Place your hand here."

"Hold your breath."

"This may squeeze a bit."

As she captured the images, I thought about ways clinics could make mammograms more pleasant. Spa music? Warm slippers?

I was having a 3D mammogram, which entailed extra pictures because of my dense breast tissue and my mom's history of breast cancer. My small breasts were stretched and smashed onto the cold metal eight times.

"I know the drill," I said casually as the technician finished. "Hope for no phone call and a report in the mail from my primary doctor."

She smiled.

"How do the images look?" I asked.

"A radiologist reads the images, I just take them," she said cheerfully.

During the drive home, I chatted with my friend Nicole about what to wear for my upcoming high school reunion that weekend.

My neighbors were headed out for a walk when I got home, so I decided to join them. Twenty minutes into the walk, a text message popped up on my phone: "MyChart has a new message for you." It was a message from the doctor's electronic health record patient portal. I took it as a good sign and planned to log in and read the message when I returned from the walk.

And then I promptly forgot.

Later, when I remembered, I struggled to access MyChart. I could almost hear Jordan telling me I should have written my login information down as I tried several combinations of usernames and passwords. When I finally got it right, I broke into a cold sweat when I saw the note:

"Need additional imaging evaluation and possible biopsy. Right breast: No suspicious findings. Left breast: There are calcifications in the upper outer breast, 4 centimeters from the nipple. Possible associated asymmetry."

Callbacks were common, I knew that, but this felt different. Did biopsies usually get scheduled with a callback? I did my best to push my worries aside. I scheduled the appointment for Friday that same week at Piper Breast Center in Minneapolis for additional tests.

The night before the appointment, I stepped into the infrared sauna in our basement that had been a

COVID splurge and turned on a recorded meditation. I managed to contort my body into legs up the wall pose within the small space, close my eyes and breathe deeply as I listened to the recording. When the meditation was done, I thought about my aunt Elaine and her little cleaning man. I imagined my own cleaning man getting rid of any malignant cells that may have been in my body as I chanted, "I am strong. I am healthy. I do not have cancer."

The next day, as Jordan and I drove to the Piper Breast Center, memories of the same drive for Mom's weekly chemo infusion sessions came flooding back. I was numb as I checked in, feeling more like a number than a person as I followed the line in front of me through the COVID screenings.

"Do you have a fever? Have you been exposed to someone with COVID in the last 14 days? Have you traveled outside the U.S. in the last 30 days? Do you have any of these symptoms?" a tired-looking receptionist asked as she handed me a checklist.

When I answered "no" to all the questions, she directed me to the fourth floor.

"Only women in the back," she said with kind eyes. Jordan would have to remain in the waiting area.

Maybe it was for the best. I was thankful Jordan

came with me, but I knew he was distracted. I could feel it deep in my bones. He would rather not be there. He would rather be working. He was most content while working. He had too much to do. I knew he saw it as a special gift he was giving me by not working for a few hours. After all, he is a doctor, and saving lives is always a priority.

I changed into a robe and padded to the women-only waiting area. I pushed away thoughts of Jordan in the lobby obsessively reading and responding to work emails and looked at my own phone hoping to be distracted. The stock market was down. The suicide rate was up. COVID cases continued to climb. Not the distraction I was hoping for. I logged on to Facebook. My feed was filled with happy smiling faces and adorable kid pics in "Class of 2022 Senior Parent Challenge" posts. Much better.

After 20 minutes of scrolling on my phone, I heard my name called.

"Let me know when you can't tolerate it anymore," the technician said. "That is when we want to take the picture." The machine would squeeze even harder and flatten my breast even more than the last mammogram. I wasn't sure how that was possible.

As she got the image, I thought of the "Choose Your Own Adventure" books I'd read as a kid, when

I would choose one direction or another and the outcome would be different. If only there was a way to look ahead in the story, to choose the direction with no cancer.

After the tech was done, she informed me the doctor would read the images right away and make recommendations for next steps.

"Would you like your husband to come back to wait with you?" she asked gently, leading me to a private room. I said I would and held back tears.

As Jordan and I waited together, the technician came back and informed us the doctor would need to do an ultrasound of my breast. I followed her to another exam room, sat on the table and began to shiver. My body was catching up with my mind.

I laid on my side and raised my arm up over my head. The technician covered me with a warm blanket and slathered my breast with warm ultrasound gel. The last time I felt that gel on my skin was during Gabi's ultrasound. I shed happy tears during that joyous moment as we saw her healthy body and watched her heartbeat. Now sad silent tears streamed down my face as I took in the doctor's serious expression.

"We can't rule anything out with the ultrasound,"

the doctor said. "We'll need to do a special biopsy that uses the mammography machine to guide it."

"What does that mean exactly?" I asked, my voice cracking, tears coming more quickly.

"You have an asymmetry on your upper left breast, and we need a sample of the tissue," she said robotically.

I would later learn an asymmetry is an area of increased density in one breast when compared to the corresponding area in the opposite breast. I felt like I was just a breast to her, a number. In that moment, she didn't seem to care that I had three children, a puppy, a husband and friends and family who loved me.

The doctor asked for my consent to do the procedure and rattled off a list of what could go wrong. I didn't hear any of it. Until she mentioned my left breast implant.

The implants were something I had fretted over more recently, as I began eliminating toxins I put on and in my body. I got them after I had finished nursing my third baby, Gabi, when she was almost 2. I was self-conscious about how deflated and saggy my breasts had become and got small saline implants the size of my pre-baby breasts. The surgeon suggested I was making a mistake with the small size. "Nine out of 10 women come back for larger breasts," he said authoritatively. I assured him I was comfortable with my decision.

A year earlier, after learning about issues women were having years after they'd gotten implants, I considered having them removed. I researched my specific implants and lot number and met with a plastic surgeon for a consult.

"It doesn't sound like you are having health issues from your implants," he said, his eyes warm with compassion. "At some point they will wear out. Why don't you wait until then?"

It sounded like a good plan. I hadn't thought about it again, until this moment, lying on my side on an exam table, my breast still sticky with ultrasound gel, the robot doctor informing me without an ounce of compassion that my left breast implant might pop during the biopsy. Burst, just like that.

Next thing I knew, a kind nurse explained what would happen during the procedure. I would sit upright and very still with my head turned to the right. She would chat with me to keep my mind off what was happening. I would feel a few pinches, a burning sensation as the numbing medication was injected.

"We will continue to inject numbing medication

while we slice—" she said. "I'm sorry—perform the biopsy."

I pictured my breast being sliced into pieces like a kiwi fruit and felt queasy.

The nurse explained the doctor would implant a tiny titanium clip in my breast to mark the tissue for future mammograms. I interrupted. I'd learned that many types of metal were bad for the body and could cause negative side effects. Would I experience any side effects from the metal? Were there any other options?

"The titanium won't hurt you; people tolerate it really well," she said, adjusting her mask. "Don't worry, you won't set off any metal detectors at the airport."

I didn't know whether to laugh or cry.

As the biopsy procedure began, I focused on a piece of paper on the cabinet in front of me and took deep breaths. The sweet nurse sat right next me, describing each step, but I wasn't really listening; I was focused on keeping myself calm.

"I am strong. I am healthy. I do not have cancer. Fuck cancer," I repeated in my mind. I believed my body was receiving the message. I believed my cells were listening.

"You will hear a loud pop," the nurse said,

startling me out of my thoughts. "Stay very still please ... you shouldn't feel a thing."

When she announced the procedure was done, I began to shiver uncontrollably again.

"May I have another warm blanket?" I asked.

"You can change back into your everyday clothes now," the nurse said.

This definitely didn't feel like "everyday."

Since it was Friday afternoon, the biopsy results would not be available until Monday afternoon. The weekend was filled with activities I hoped would be a distraction, and they started that evening. Ages ago, I had planned to meet Jen, one of my best friends from high school, at the homecoming football game, where my senior, Sage, who was attending the same high school I graduated from three decades earlier, would sing "The Star-Spangled Banner" at the kick-off of the game. Afterwards, Jen and I would head to our 30-year high school reunion party together.

For a brief moment, I considered changing plans. But I wasn't about to miss Sage's singing. There was no point staying home to stress and worry. My trembling nerves had calmed, and my breast was completely numb.

I called the salon that was a mile from my house. "Is anyone available to blow out my hair?" I asked hopefully. I wanted to feel normal and pretty. I wanted to feel like Cinderella at the ball, even if the ball was a high school homecoming game and reunion.

The evening was indeed a great distraction. Jen and I had a wonderful time catching up. As I drove home, I realized the numbness had worn off and my breast was throbbing. I wondered what my classmates would think if next week they heard I had breast cancer. "I just saw Marnie at the reunion! She was smiling and laughing and looked so healthy!" I imagined them exclaiming in disbelief to one another.

At home, I undressed and examined my naked body in the mirror. My left breast was black, blue and yellow and swollen like it was engorged with milk. It looked the same as when I had mastitis back when I nursed Zach. I never thought my breasts would recover back then. More battle scars, I thought. Each wound told its own story.

I took an Aleve and attempted to sleep. I tossed and turned most of the night. Every position was uncomfortable. The next morning, I was sore and crabby. The pain in my breast was compounded by the effects of drinking cheap red wine immediately following the 10-day liver detox program I did with my clients quarterly. But there was no time to wallow—there were many activities that day and evening. Sage and Gabi were both going to the high school homecoming dance. There would be group photos of them with their friends, and then Jordan and I would head to a surprise 50th birthday party for a friend.

I was excited about the surprise party. We were gathering with a close group of friends who were all couples. We named our core group of three couples MAD Productions, combining the first letters of our last names. We had met when our kids had all become friends in elementary school and took turns hosting dinner parties with our families. At the parties, after a delicious meal and fun conversation, the adults would sink into the sofas completely satiated and slightly drunk and watch as our kids performed elaborate, impromptu musical productions like "Into the Woods," "Wicked" and "Les Misérables," complete with singing and thrown together costumes.

Our families had taken ski trips together to Lutsen Mountains in Northern Minnesota near the Canadian border. In 2017, we took a MAD Productions trip to Tuscany, Italy, with just the adults. We dubbed ourselves Siamo Sei, which translates to "we are six" in Italian. We chose Italian nicknames: La Marna and Giordano; the other couples were Davido Primo and Steffi, and Aimeé and Il Professore. We rented a farmhouse on top of a hill with views of rolling green vineyards and the medieval towers of Montepulciano and Montalcino just visible in the distance. We spent our days strolling through small towns, enjoying leisurely lunches, visiting wineries and sampling delicious local red wines.

Our evenings were spent at the farmhouse where we shared amazing dinners. One night, we cooked a multi-course meal together with the guidance of two Italian chefs who showed us how to make pasta and tiramisu from scratch. Flour and egg on our faces and up to our elbows. My normally gluten-free lifestyle out the window.

"Alora! I ragazzi!" which translates roughly to "Come on, children!" the chefs implored as they smiled and laughed along with us. Three hours later, we sat down to an unbelievable multi-course meal we had cooked together.

"Let's send for the kids," Aimeé joked, though she also meant it.

No one was ready to go home. It was a once-in-a-lifetime trip that cemented an already strong bond.

I hadn't mentioned to any of them I might have cancer.

The surprise party that night was for Il Professore (also known as David). I dressed in a black Amanda

Uprichard jumpsuit I'd ordered online a few days earlier, before I thought I might have cancer. I looked at myself in the mirror. No one would suspect I might have cancer. I squinted, as if it might help me see inside myself. I couldn't see the growing sense of gloom I felt in my gut. "I do not have cancer. I do not have cancer," I chanted and turned away from my reflection. I ordered myself to enjoy the evening and I did. Celebrating life with friends was the perfect distraction. As we ate and drank and roasted and toasted David, the dread in my belly was replaced by the ache of laughter.

The next morning, I cried until my eyes were red and swollen and my face was blotchy. I vacillated between thoughts of "What if I have cancer?" and "I do not have cancer!" The day dragged on—it was the longest Sunday of my life. I was thankful for my mom who listened as I cried on the phone, and for my best girlfriends, Nicole and Jessica, who knew I needed a distraction and insisted we take a long walk.

I canceled my meetings on Monday and planned to stay by the phone for the biopsy results. I did not want to miss a call from the doctor. I jumped each time I received a text or phone call. The few family members and friends I'd shared the news with were reaching out, asking if I'd gotten the results. I didn't respond. I couldn't. I would let them know the moment I heard something.

Lila and I went for a long walk on our favorite trail. Beneath the golden and red trees, I breathed in the earthy smell of autumn. It was another gorgeous, sunny day and I prayed to the universe, the trees, the birds and whoever and whatever was listening to me: "Please, do not let me have cancer."

Around 3:30 p.m., my caller ID displayed the name of the hospital where the Piper Breast Center was located. As I raced up the stairs to take it in my office, I caught my foot on the step and fell flat on my face as I answered.

"Hello!" I shouted, out of breath.

"Hi Marnie," came the voice of sweet nurse who'd been with me for the biopsy, only she sounded concerned. "The radiologists are backed up and haven't reviewed your films yet. They may get to it this evening, but the office staff leaves at 4 p.m., so we won't be able to give you your results today. I am so sorry."

"You promised me I would hear today!" I exploded.

"I am so sorry," she repeated. "It is out of my control. You will have the results by noon tomorrow."

She spoke softly, as if trying to calm a child who was having a tantrum.

I felt like having a tantrum. I wanted to punch and kick and scream.

"Is it possible the results will be online tonight in MyChart?" I asked hopefully.

"It's possible, but it's best if they are reviewed by a doctor first," she said.

I pictured her shutting down her computer, putting on her jacket, disconnecting from work for the evening while I obsessed about my test results all night.

An hour later, a received a text from MyChart that said there was an update to my chart. I told Jordan—he was a doctor; he could review the chart with me. I raced to my computer, logged in, and held my breath.

"Negative for malignancy!" I screamed, grabbing Jordan's arms, jumping up and down with him the way we'd always done when we were excited about something.

I am strong! I am healthy! I do not have cancer! Happy tears came then. I was profoundly grateful. I would not take anything for granted.

CHAPTER FIFTEEN

**My mission in life is not merely to
survive, but to thrive.
—MAYA ANGELOU**

Baubie was the matriarch of our family. She had
anointed herself "The Queen of Everything" years
ago and had it painted on the wall above the head of
her bed. She was one of the feistiest people I knew.
It was her way or the highway. In her younger years,
she had short curly red hair and big glasses that
matched her big, warm smile and deep throaty laugh.
Later, she skipped the perms and let her hair go gray,
wearing it in a short, straight bob just below her ears.
This was quite a shift from decades of weekly beauty
salon visits. In those days, she never wanted to go
out in the snow, wind or rain for fear that her new
hairdo would get ruined. Sometimes, when she had
no choice, she would tie on what she referred to as a
"schmatta"—a head rag or scarf—to protect her hair.

She tended to favor the boys in our family, but
I was the first granddaughter. And my brother and I
were the children of her oldest son of seven children,

so we had the benefit of being in the first wave of grandkids and having grandparents who were young and full of energy.

Baubie taught me to play Gin Rummy and Rummikub, and we often played for hours at a time.

Baubie found great joy in baking. She was a master baker. Her specialties were lemon poppy seed cookies, Mandel bread, banana bread, potato knishes and rugelach.

"Baubie, what kind of banana bread did you make?" I'd ask whenever I visited, my eyes twinkling.

"What do you mean what kind? There is only one way to make banana bread—with no chocolate chips!" she would scold.

Even in her 90s she continued to bake, or she would instruct her caregivers to bake her recipes, so when family came to visit, she could offer us a loaf of banana bread or something sweet to take home. She baked certain items for certain people and would get protective over who got what, especially her poppy seed cookies.

"You can't have those! They are Noah's favorite! I made them just for him!"

My mom was not a baker, so the little baking I did, I learned from Baubie. When I was a young adult, I had no interest in it. I never liked how precisely all the ingredients had to be measured. It seemed too much like chemistry class to me. I preferred to cook, adding a sprinkle of this and a dash of that, often improvising my way into a meal. As I got older, though I was still not a huge fan of baking, I wanted to learn some family recipes. I wanted my own daughters, who are better bakers than I am, to learn alongside me.

One afternoon during the pandemic, my daughters and I spent four hours making potato knishes from scratch. We were using Baubie's recipe, but video calls with her were a challenge, so we FaceTimed my aunt Toni.

"How do you roll it out?" I asked my aunt after trying unsuccessfully to flatten the dough without a rolling pin, my arms exhausted from my feeble attempts.

"What?!" Aunt Toni exclaimed. "You've been married all these years and you don't own a rolling pin?!"

Baubie was just as surprised when she later learned I had no rolling pin.

In addition to her knack for baking and winning games, my Baubie had always been the most positive person I knew. She passed this trait down to my dad who still says "I'm the best in the Midwest" when anyone asks him how he's doing, and he passed it down to me. I have often wondered if it was nature or nurture that influenced the way we have all approached our lives with such positive spirits. Baubie's glass was always half full. This was despite being the child of divorced parents, and having an alcoholic father during a time when such things were taboo and kept quiet. She had been through a lot of heartache in her 90-plus years, but she didn't let it get her down.

"I hold my innermost thoughts close to my heart," she told me once, when I asked if she confided in her girlfriends. "I have family to share my problems with, and one close friend, and that's all you need." I wasn't sure I agreed with this sentiment and wondered if she had missed out on the joy of deep friendships. "No one wants to hear your drama anyway," she added with authority.

Having grown up during the Depression, she was a saver, nothing could go to waste, not one scrap of anything. I learned to graciously accept whatever well-loved cast-off item she wanted to pass on; I would decide what to do with it later. Most often, those items were discarded or donated. Still, I felt like I was lightening Baubie's load.

Baubie was known for saying, "You must

celebrate everything, even the small things!" She loved a good party and being at the center of it. For her 90th birthday, we held a big party in her honor, and all our out-of-town family flew to Minneapolis for it. Leading up to it, Zach, who was 14 at the time, spent months learning and practicing George Gershwin's difficult piece, "Rhapsody in Blue," on the piano. Baubie had recently declared it her favorite song of all time and it was Zach's gift to his great-grandmother. We were all in tears during this beautiful moment.

Zach also accompanied several of my uncles, cousins, Sage, Gabi and me on the piano as we performed "Seasons of Love" from the Broadway musical "Rent" at the party. In that moment, surrounded by family, I didn't think about my voice. I just sang the song from my heart for Baubie, loudly, proudly, unleashed. I let my voice meld into the other beautiful voices and the love surrounding me.

Now, whenever I hear "Seasons of Love," tears spring to my eyes and I feel the urge to belt out the lyrics. Those words carry so much meaning and remind me how proud I am to be a member of my strong Dachis family.

In the spring of 2020, Stephanie and I went to Baubie's condo on her 96th birthday to interview her for our podcast. It was the height of the pandemic, so we set up our recording gear on two card tables in the backyard of the brown brick building. Baubie had been released from a transitional care facility three weeks earlier, after recovering from a broken hip, which in itself was no small feat for someone her age. No one would have known by how quickly she shuffled toward us with her walker, her caretaker beside her. She looked beautiful in pink—her favorite color—and I felt so lucky to be there, once again celebrating her special day.

We blew kisses through our masks, and she took a seat in front of the microphone at the opposite end of the tables where Stephanie and I sat, with a 10-foot gap between us. We hadn't considered it might be difficult for her to hear us with the distance and through surgical grade masks, but we proceeded as planned. We had a wonderful conversation and Baubie shared some of her secrets for living a long and happy life:

Think positively.

Always reflect on how you can do better.

Be kind to others.

Find joy in the little things in each day.

"And what does the art of living well mean to you?" I asked as we wrapped up.

"Family first in every way. Being a good person, helping out whenever you can. And enjoying everything—nature, your family, your friends, your children, your grandchildren and great-grandchildren. All that is important in your life, and I think with that, you can't live any better."

Through tears, Stephanie and I nodded and agreed. I was so proud she was my grandmother.

A little over a year later, in December 2021, Baubie joined us for a family vacation in Mexico. She led a walker-friendly dance party in the hotel lobby, which attracted the attention of several other guests who joined in on the fun. She was also determined to take a soak in the hot tub, so our mission became getting "Baubie in the tubbie." With her can-do attitude and the dedication of the group, we made it happen. Every moment of that trip was a wonderful celebration with her.

A few months later, in May 2022, my family gathered at Baubie's condo just before her death. The outside world stopped. We were present with her and with each other. We took turns holding her hands, rubbing her feet, and talking and singing to her in the hope she could hear us. We were there for days, sharing stories and meals. One minute laughing, the next minute crying. We surrounded her with love so she could leave this earth the way she wished.

Baubie passed away just after Mother's Day, and just shy of her 98th birthday.

"I want to speak at Baubie's funeral," I asserted to my family of 35, all crammed into Baubie's family room after she passed.

Many strong personalities were involved in planning Baubie's funeral, everyone had an opinion, and everyone expected my brother Louie to speak on behalf of the grandchildren. He was the eloquent one and the eldest. But something was pulling me to honor her publicly, to use my voice. So on that day in her stifling apartment, I advocated for myself. My face was so hot, it felt like it was melting.

I spent the next few days reflecting on the enormous impact she had had on my life. I thought about her "Baubie-isms": "There's no such thing as bored" and "There's no sick allowed" were two of her favorites. And if she called you a "bauk" (which wasn't Yiddish, just pure Baubie), it meant something like "You are an idiot, but I still love you."

On the day of her funeral, I woke to the familiar sound of birdsong and recalled how Baubie knew the names of most birds and plants on sight. The weather that day was gorgeous.

At the synagogue, as I walked to the podium, gripping my pages, I took deep breaths and reminded myself "You can do this." What I had to say was important. I needed to share my words for Baubie and for myself. I adjusted the microphone and inhaled a deep, calming breath.

"To my Baubie who loved me dearly …" I said loudly from the front of the room.

I looked out at the hundreds of family members and friends there to honor her. I didn't think about my voice. I only thought about Baubie and paying tribute to her. No restraints, no resistance. And then I confidently shared the words on my pages. Not once did I falter.

I finished by telling her, "I have looked up to you from the time I was a little girl. You were my role model extraordinaire. I am the luckiest girl in the world to have had you in my life for 49 years." I said I knew she was with Zadie now, and I sent my love and a hug. "I will never forget you. You are always with me, in my heart and soul."

ACKNOWLEDGMENTS

From the time I was a little girl, I have wanted to write a book. A teacher once told me, "If you write, you are a writer," and it stuck with me. I journaled for years, and in fact, re-read many of my old journals while writing this book. I envisioned writing a novel in my earlier years, and then later, when my mom was undergoing cancer treatment, I set out to write a nonfiction book about strong women cancer survivors and thrivers, telling their stories through an alternative wellness lens. After a year on the project, I set that book aside. But I will never forget the many women I interviewed, their heart-filled stories, and their powerful messages about life.

In the fall of 2019, I enrolled in a writing class. It rekindled my desire to write a book, and the rest is history. I felt so much pride and joy throughout this process, and I am grateful I was fortunate to have the time, resources, inspiration and space to write this book.

I am profoundly grateful to the people who helped me bring this book to life. Many family and friends who have been a part of my journey appear in this book; a fair number do not. Either way, I have felt your love and support throughout, and I appreciate the impact you have had on my life.

To my CNF Foundation faculty and classmates: Without your guidance and support, this book would not exist.

To Joelle Fraser: I participated in your 30-Minute Memoir course four times. You pushed and encouraged me in a way that made me want to continue to write. It was tough, and some days I had no idea what I would write about. The weekly deadlines and feedback were incredibly helpful, and I don't think this book would have come to fruition without your encouragement and constructive feedback.

To Kate Hopper, my developmental editor extraordinaire: Your encouragement, support, guidance and honesty were invaluable and helped me shape what the book is today. I loved working with you and learning about your life along the way. You forced me to dig deeply at times when I really didn't want to. You are so easy to work with, and I hope to have an opportunity to work together again.

To Chris Olsen, Leslie Lagerstrom and the team at Publish Her Press: Thank you for helping me turn my manuscript into an actual book, opening my eyes to the publishing process, caring about the quality of the books you publish, and helping to make the process as smooth as possible.

To my yoga gurus: There are so many of you who have impacted me along the way. You touch so many lives, including mine, and the ripple effect you leave on this earth is beautiful.

To my teachers and mentors at IIN and IHP: Thanks for inspiring me to be healthy, heal myself from within, strive for longevity, deviate from societal norms, and share my knowledge with others.

To Stephanie Potter, co-host of "The Art of Living Well Podcast": Thank you for your friendship and partnership, for our Monday morning chats, for giving me the space to vent when I need to, and your positivity and support.

To guests of "The Art of Living Well Podcast": I have learned so much from our shared experience, and each of you has been a teacher in some way, shape or form.

To my wonderful Dachis, Marmet and Rosten family members: I know how lucky I am to have each and every one of you in my life. The support and love I feel surrounding me from all of you is a wonderful security that I hold near and dear to my heart.

To my treasured girlfriends: You know who you are. Though some of you are not mentioned in this book, it is only because the book focuses on certain aspects of my life. It does not lessen how incredibly important you are to me. I am forever grateful to all of you for your friendship and unwavering support—the ups, the downs, the fun, the laughs. There is nothing like girlfriends!

To Mom and Dad: You have shaped so much of who I am today. Thank you for supporting and loving me unconditionally. I am forever grateful to you.

To Jordan, my best friend, my partner in crime and my love: You are the only person on this earth who knows me as well as you do. We have grown up together and have been on this journey of life with one another longer than we have not. Your support and guidance in this process has been invaluable. Thank you for letting me share some of our story in this book.

To my kiddos, Zach, Sage and Gabi: Thank you for giving me the gift and honor of motherhood, by far my favorite role. You enrich my life in ways I never imagined, and you inspire me to be a better person. My love for you three is boundless. Thank you for letting me write about you, and thanks for all the love and laughter along the way. Keep being true to you!

ABOUT THE AUTHOR

Marnie Dachis Marmet is an author, serial entrepreneur, board-certified health coach and the founder of Zenful Life Coaching, a practice dedicated to helping women and teens create a healthier and happier life. She supports clients in implementing personalized nutrition and wellness plans and making gradual, sustainable lifestyle changes. Her areas of expertise include longevity, mind-body-spirit holistic health, gut health, yoga, mindfulness and meditation. As co-creator and co-host of "The Art of Living Well Podcast," Marnie empowers listeners to challenge the status quo, and she provides information and inspiration for living their healthiest and most authentic life. She has also owned and operated ChillyBean Promotions, a promotional products company, for more than 20 years.

Marnie lives in Minnesota, where she enjoys an active lifestyle, traveling, photography, reading and spending time with family, friends and her labradoodle, Lila.